MY WELLBEING JOURNEY 3

Junior Cycle SPHE

Catherine Deegan
& Edel O'Brien

Gill Education
Hume Avenue
Park West
Dublin 12
www.gilleducation.ie

Gill Education is an imprint of M.H. Gill & Co.

© Catherine Deegan and Edel O'Brien 2019

ISBN: 978-0-7171-84309

Design: Síofra Murphy

Illustrations: Oxford Designers & Illustrators, Derry Dillon

At the time of going to press, all web addresses were active and contained information relevant to the topics in this book. Gill Education does not, however, accept responsibility for the content or views contained on these websites. Content, views and addresses may change beyond the publisher or author's control. Students should always be supervised when reviewing websites.

The authors and publisher are grateful to the following for permission to reproduce copyrighted material:

'I will fall for someone who' © Edel O'Brien, 2019. 'The Thickness of Ice' © Liz Loxley.

For permission to reproduce photographs, the authors and publisher gratefully acknowledge the following:

Courtesy of Al-Anon Family Groups UK & Eire: 211; © Alamy: 14T, 56B, 56CR, 56T, 92C, 92CR, 92TL, 92TR, 93C, 93CL, 93CR, 93TCL, 93TCR, 93TL, 93TR, 94, 95C, 95CL, 95CR, 95T, 157, 173T, 175BL, 175BR, 176, 177; Courtesy of Aware: 210; Courtesy of BeLonG To Youth Services: 211; Courtesy of Bodywhys: 211; Courtesy of Childline, The Irish Society for the Prevention of Cruelty to Children (ISPCC): 210; © Digital Vision: 32, 87CB; Courtesy of Dublin's 98FM: 173; © E+: 14TC, 55, 87T, 114B, 208; © EyeEm: 88CL; © iStock: 1, 14BC, 14B, 18, 20, 21, 31, 33, 56CL, 61, 70, 87C, 87B, 88T, 88CT, 92CL, 100, 101, 106, 114T, 114C, 115, 119, 126, 132, 133, 143, 149, 154, 156, 158, 160, 166, 173CR, 174, 175T, 181, 182, 190, 192, 204, 205, 206; Courtesy of Jigsaw, National Centre for Youth Mental Health (CLG): 211; Courtesy of Raidió Teilifís Éireann: 173; Courtesy of Rainbows Ireland: 210; Courtesy of Samaritans Ireland: 210; Courtesy of Spin1038: 173; © Shutterstock: 93TC, 121, 123, 140; Courtesy of Snapchat: 173; Courtesy of St. Vincent de Paul: 210; Courtesy of The HSE Sexual Health and Crisis Pregnancy Programme: 210.

The authors and publisher have made every effort to trace all copyright holders, but if any have been inadvertently overlooked we would be pleased to make the necessary arrangement at the first opportunity.

CONTENTS

INTRODUCTION to *My Wellbeing Journey 3*

Welcome to *My Wellbeing Journey 3*! We hope you have enjoyed following this programme over the last two years and that it has helped you to learn more about and prioritise your health and wellbeing!

SPHE supports each of the six indicators of Wellbeing:

 active responsible connected resilient respected aware

For that reason, SPHE and *My Wellbeing Journey* contributes significantly to your school's Wellbeing programme.

SPHE gives you the chance to develop a positive sense of self and the skills and insights for caring for yourself and others. You'll learn to make informed decisions about health and wellbeing and you will develop the resilience needed to cope with some of the challenges of the teenage years.

SPHE and *My Wellbeing Journey* put you at the centre of the learning experience. The active learning methods used throughout this series encourage you to engage fully with the topics discussed. We hope that the activities presented in *My Wellbeing Journey* will make for fun, thought-provoking and valuable SPHE classes.

Catherine Deegan and Edel O'Brien

Using *My Wellbeing Journey 3*

Specification links

My Wellbeing Journey is clearly linked to the SPHE specification. Not only is the book broken into four colour-coded strands but each lesson is linked to a specific Learning Outcome and Wellbeing Indicator. Learning Outcomes are then broken down further into student-friendly learning intentions.

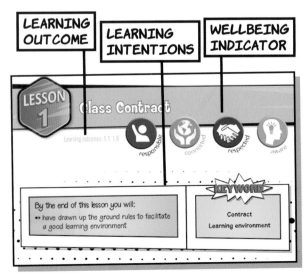

This very clear curriculum mapping will support planning. It will also assist the assessment process as you need to make sure that the Classroom-Based Assessment is based on Learning Outcomes from more than one strand.

Development of Key Skills

Each activity in the book supports the development of at least one of the Junior Cycle Key Skills. Icons indicate which Key Skill is addressed.

 Being Literate
 Communicating
 Being Creative
 Managing Information
 Managing Myself
 Being Numerate
 Wellness
 Working with Others

Meanwhile the words underneath the icon show what element or aspect of the Key Skill is being developed.

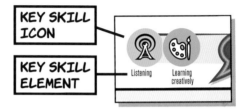

Reflection

Reflecting on learning is an important aspect of the Junior Cycle Framework. The Learning Keepsakes at the end of each lesson provide scaffolding for regular reflection. These reflections are particularly useful when it comes to deciding on a CBA in Second or Third Year and for supporting communication with parents. Additional Topic Reviews are available on GillExplore and provide more opportunities for reflection.

Assessment

Meet the Challenges, linked to specific Learning Outcomes, Key Skills and Wellbeing Indicators and with clear success criteria, help prepare you for the Classroom-Based Assessment. They are particularly intended for people following the SPHE Short Course but provide engaging assessment opportunities for all SPHE students. A special Assessment section at the start of this book will also guide you through the process of completing a successful CBA.

Additional resources

Numerous resources (including videos and PowerPoints) which support teaching and learning in SPHE are included on GillExplore.ie. The *My Wellbeing Journey Teacher's Resource Book* includes useful lesson planning material and schemes of work.

Following the SPHE course using *My Wellbeing Journey*

Your school has a choice in how it implements SPHE. You can:

- stick with the older modular SPHE curriculum (70 hours), first rolled out in 2000

- follow the newer SPHE short course (100 hours), developed under the new Junior Cycle Framework in 2016

- develop your own, purpose-built SPHE short course that meets requirements (e.g. is at least 70 hours long, includes RSE).

All of the choices can seem quite confusing but the *My Wellbeing Journey* series is flexible so it can be used whatever option you take. The series fully covers both the NCCA-developed modular and short courses. All activities in *My Wellbeing Journey* specifically nurture different Key Skill elements, while all lessons are mapped to relevant Statements of Learning and Wellbeing Indicators, to help ensure you are in line with the Junior Cycle Framework.

How *My Wellbeing Journey 3* helps you fulfil the Learning Outcomes of the SPHE Short Course

The table below highlights where the various Learning Outcomes are addressed in this book. This list of Learning Outcomes is also important as you will need to make sure that your CBA addresses Learning Outcomes from at least two different strands.

STRAND 1: WHO AM I?

STUDENTS SHOULD BE ABLE TO	RELEVANT LESSONS
1.1 appreciate the importance of building their own self-esteem and that of others	Lesson 1
1.2 welcome individual difference based on an appreciation of their own uniqueness	See *My Wellbeing Journey 1*
1.3 participate in informed discussions about the impact of physical, emotional, psychological and social development in adolescence	Lesson 10
1.4 recognise how sexuality and gender identity is part of what it means to be human and has biological, psychological, cultural, social and spiritual dimensions	Lesson 10
1.5 identify short, medium and long-term personal goals and ways in which they might be achieved	Lessons 2, 3, 4, 5
1.6 apply decision-making skills in a variety of situations	Lessons 7, 8, 9
1.7 source appropriate and reliable information about health and wellbeing	Lesson 6
1.8 explain how stereotyping can contribute to a person's understanding and experience of rights and wellbeing	See *My Wellbeing Journey 1* and *2*
1.9 appreciate the importance of respectful and inclusive behaviour in promoting a safe environment free from bias and discrimination	Lesson 1

STRAND 2: MINDING MYSELF AND OTHERS

STUDENTS SHOULD BE ABLE TO	RELEVANT LESSONS
2.1 evaluate how diet, physical activity, sleep/rest and hygiene contribute to self-confidence, self-esteem and wellbeing	Lessons 15, 17, 31
2.2 critique the impact of the media, advertising and other influences on one's decisions about health and wellbeing	Lesson 16
2.3 describe what promotes a sense of belonging in school, at home and in the wider community and their own role in creating an inclusive environment	See *My Wellbeing Journey 2*
2.4 distinguish between appropriate care giving and receiving	Lesson 18
2.5 demonstrate the personal and social skills to address pressure to smoke, to drink alcohol and/or use other substances	Lesson 19
2.6 reflect on the personal, social and legal consequences of their own or others' drug use	Lesson 19
2.7 critique information and supports available for young people in relation to substance use	Lesson 19
2.8 use the skills of active listening and responding appropriately in a variety of contexts	Lesson 11
2.9 use good communication skills to respond to criticism and conflict	Lessons 12, 13, 14
2.10 describe appropriate responses to incidents of bullying	See *My Wellbeing Journey 1* and *2*
2.11 appraise the roles of participants and bystanders in incidents of bullying	See *My Wellbeing Journey 1* and *2*
2.12 review the school's anti-bullying policy and internet safety guidelines explaining the implications for students' behaviour and personal safety	See *My Wellbeing Journey 2*

STRAND 3: TEAM UP

STUDENTS SHOULD BE ABLE TO	RELEVANT LESSONS
3.1 establish what young people value in different relationships and how this changes over time	Lesson 22
3.2 evaluate attitudes, skills and values that help to make, maintain and end friendships respectfully	See *My Wellbeing Journey 1* and *2*
3.3 recognise their capacity to extend and receive friendship	Lesson 20
3.4 explain the different influences on relationships and levels of intimacy	Lessons 21, 24
3.5 analyse relationship difficulties experienced by young people	Lessons 21, 22, 23, 24
3.6 describe fertility, conception, pre-natal development and birth, and the particular health considerations for each	See *My Wellbeing Journey 1* and *2*
3.7 explain what it means to take care of their sexual health	Lessons 25, 26
3.8 demonstrate assertive communication skills in support of responsible, informed decision-making about relationships and sexual health that are age and developmentally appropriate	Lessons 26, 27
3.9 reflect on the personal and social dimensions of sexual orientation and gender identity	See *My Wellbeing Journey 1* and *2*
3.10 critically analyse the use of sexual imagery and gender stereotyping in various forms of media	Lesson 28
3.11 critique the influence of media on their understanding of sexuality and sexual health	Lesson 28

STRAND 4: MY MENTAL HEALTH

STUDENTS SHOULD BE ABLE TO	RELEVANT LESSONS
4.1 explain what it means to have positive mental health	See *My Wellbeing Journey 1*
4.2 appreciate the importance of talking things over, including recognising the links between thoughts, feelings and behaviour	Lessons 29, 30
4.3 practise some relaxation techniques	Lesson 30, 31
4.4 participate in an informed discussion about mental health issues experienced by young people and/or their friends and family	See *My Wellbeing Journey 1* and *2*
4.5 appreciate what it means to live with mental ill-health	Lesson 32
4.6 critique mental health services available to young people locally	Lesson 33
4.7 explain the significance of substance use for one's mental health	Lesson 19
4.8 practise a range of strategies for building resilience	Lesson 30
4.9 use coping skills for managing life's challenges	Lesson 30
4.10 explain the wide range of life events where they might experience loss and bereavement	See *My Wellbeing Journey 1*
4.11 outline the personal, social, emotional and physical responses to loss and bereavement	See *My Wellbeing Journey 1* and *2*
4.12 compare how loss and bereavement are portrayed in a variety of contexts and cultures	See *My Wellbeing Journey 2*
4.13 describe how they might care for themselves and be supportive of others in times of loss or bereavement	See *My Wellbeing Journey 1* and *2*

How *My Wellbeing Journey 3* helps you fulfil the SPHE Modular Curriculum

The older SPHE modular curriculum is prepared in ten modules, each of which appears in each year of the three-year cycle. Your school can still follow the modular course, if it prefers. However, if you are following the modular curriculum, you'll need to make sure that you are integrating key aspects of the Junior Cycle Framework, such as Statements of Learning, Key Skills and Wellbeing Indicators. As *My Wellbeing Journey* is written to be fully in line with the Junior Cycle Framework, all of this integration has been done for you.

MODULE	RELEVANT LESSONS
Belonging and Integrating	Lessons 1, 2
Self-Management: A sense of purpose	Lessons 3, 4, 5
Communication Skills	Lessons 11, 12, 13, 14
Physical Health	Lessons 15, 17, 31
Friendship	Lesson 20
Relationships and Sexuality	Lessons 10, 21, 22, 23, 24, 25
Emotional Health	Lessons 29, 30
Influences and Decisions	Lesson 7
Substance Use	Lesson 19
Personal Safety	Lessons 8, 9, 33

Additional lessons: 6, 16, 18, 26, 27, 28, 32. These lessons have been written to fulfil the requirements of the new SPHE Short Course. If you are following the modular course you mightn't have time to cover these new lessons and the additional assessment options (Meet the Challenges) provided in the book. Feel free to cover these lessons, if your context allows.

Assessment

If you are following the SPHE Short Course, your learning will be assessed in the form of one **Classroom-Based Assessment (CBA)**. This CBA can take place in either **Second or Third Year**, once you have completed learning in at least three strands. The outcome of your SPHE CBA will be reported on your **Junior Cycle Profile of Achievement**.

Classroom-Based Assessment: Advice for students

✔ **Choose a project that you are interested in learning more about.** If you are doing a group project, try to ensure that each member of the group is interested and cares about the topic being addressed.

✔ **Keep a record of the topics that interest you** as you go through the different strands of the SPHE short course. You can do this by completing your Learning Keepsakes and Topic Reviews. Look out for images, videos and written materials that will help you to learn more about this topic(s). These will also help you to make your project more interesting.

✔ **Your project will focus on learning in at least two strands of the SPHE short course.** Your book is broken into four strands, each differentiated by colour. It is a good idea to begin by making links between topics in the different strands. This will help you to choose a worthwhile project.

✔ When your teacher is helping you and your classmates to decide on a project for your CBA, **use information you have already gathered and do some further research to help you** encourage your group/class to consider doing the project that you think is **worthwhile**.

✔ Once the focus of the project has been decided, **identify sources of reliable information with your teacher**.

✔ **Divide the project tasks out** between the group in such a way that everybody can work to their strengths.

✔ **Use your creativity in both capturing and presenting your project.** You can complete your project as a document, a presentation, a video and/or through images.

✔ Your teacher will support you in planning and completing your project for the SPHE CBA.

✔ The **Features of Quality** will be used to provide you with feedback about **what you are doing well and what you can do to improve**.

✔ **Keep notes on what you are learning** as you complete the CBA by filling out the **Planning and Preparation template** on the following pages. These notes will help you complete a quality reflection about your learning in the project.

Sample Projects for Classroom-Based Assessments
(adapted from www.curriculumonline.ie)

Here are some examples that might help you to come up with a project for your SPHE CBA. You might also look to the **Meet the Challenges** in your books for some inspiration!

PROJECT	STRANDS AND LEARNING OUTCOMES	SUCCESS CRITERIA
Sample 1 Design a resource for your peers called 'Aid to Decision-Making'.	**Strand 1:** 1.5, 1.6, 1.7 **Strand 2:** 2.1, 2.6, 2.7	1. Decide on the type of resource you will make. 2. Identify what materials and resources you will need for your resource. 3. Include a decision-making model or steps for making a good decision in your resource. 4. Highlight the important areas where good decision-making is important for young people, e.g. diet, substance use, studying, etc. 5. Include the names of organisations, websites and/or helplines that have information on the topics you are focusing on. 6. Decide on a format for your resource, e.g. will you make a booklet, write a blog or create a short film? 7. Use language, images, etc. that are suitable for and will appeal to young people. 8. Complete your Reflection Sheet.
Sample 2 Contribute to an advertising campaign on 'Adolescence: The age of opportunity'	**Strand 1:** 1.2, 1.4, 1.5, 1.9 **Strand 2:** 2.3, 2.5, 2.7, 2.8, 2.9, 2.10 **Strand 3:** 3.2, 3.3, 3.8, 3.9 **Strand 4:** 4.1, 4.2, 4.8, 4.9	1. Decide on the main purpose and message of your advertising campaign. 2. Decide on your audience and how best to get the message out to them. 3. Consider whether you might create a print/online/radio or TV campaign. 4. Outline some of the changes that occur in adolescence, e.g. new school, meeting new people, more responsibility, more freedom, new experiences, etc. 5. Give the advantages and challenges involved in some of these changes, e.g. being accepted, making new friends, assessments and tests, following your interests, peer pressure, etc. 6. Outline the skills adolescents can develop to meet the challenges they face, e.g. good communication skills, building their self-esteem, etc. 7. Provide the names of helplines and information sites for young people.
Sample 3 Design a media campaign about the consequences of alcohol and tobacco use and where and how to get help for drug-related problems	**Strand 2:** 2.5, 2.6, 2.7 **Strand 4:** 4.7, 4.8, 4.9	1. Decide who your target audience is. 2. Develop the key messages of your campaign. 3. Consider how you will best get your message across. Your campaign might include interviews, articles, short documentaries, viral social media clips, publicising important research or getting endorsements from well-known people. 4. Research relevant helping organisations. 5. Outline the different pressures that young people feel around substance abuse. 6. Highlight consequences of substance misuse, e.g. personal, social and legal.

Features of Quality

Your CBA will be assessed according to the following **Features of Quality**. Your teacher(s) will assign a descriptor to your CBA depending on what description best fits your CBA. It is a good idea to familiarise yourself with the Features of Quality.

DESCRIPTOR	FEATURES OF QUALITY FOR SPHE PROJECT AND REFLECTION
Exceptional	• The project reflects excellent use of background information. • It demonstrates an excellent level of creativity and original interpretation of the material. • It shows excellent awareness of audience, where this is relevant to the project. • There is substantial evidence of meaningful reflection on their learning.
Above expectations	• The project reflects very clear use of background information. • It demonstrates a very high level of creativity and original interpretation of the material. • It shows a clear awareness of audience, where this is relevant to the project. • There is strong evidence of meaningful reflection on their learning.
In line with expectations	• The project reflects satisfactory use of background information. • It demonstrates a satisfactory level of creativity in the design of the project. • It shows satisfactory awareness of audience, where this is relevant to the project. • There is good evidence of reflection on their learning.
Yet to meet expectations	• The project reflects a limited understanding of the background information. • Creativity or an ability to interpret the material in the design of the project is missing. • It lacks an awareness of audience, where this is relevant to the project. • There is little evidence of reflection on their learning.

Classroom-Based Assessment Planning and Preparation template

Fill in the following template as you plan and carry out your CBA. Doing this will help ensure you address all Features of Quality and produce an interesting and meaningful CBA.

A. Deciding on a project

First list the topics that you found most interesting in your SPHE class:

_____

_____

Look back at the four strands covered in SPHE (have a look at the contents pages in your books if you're unsure of what topics fall under which strands). Then tick which strands you would like to cover as part of your CBA:

- ☐ Strand 1: Who Am I?
- ☐ Strand 2: Minding Myself & Minding Others
- ☐ Strand 3: Team Up
- ☐ Strand 4: My Mental Health

Now list the specific learning outcomes you would like to address in your CBA. Make sure you include at least one learning outcome from two different strands. You'll find the relevant learning outcomes listed at the start of each lesson and also in a table at the front of the book.

_____

What would you like to achieve through your CBA?

_____

How will you present your information/project? Tick the relevant box or describe below.

- ☐ Advertising campaign
- ☐ Media campaign
- ☐ Display board
- ☐ Presentation
- ☐ Event
- ☐ Poster/Infographic
- ☐ Video
- ☐ Podcast
- ☐ Publication (booklet, book, magazine, newsletter)
- ☐ Other: _____

How will you divide up the work involved in the project?

_____

_____

Describe your particular role in the project:

_____

_____

_____

B. Gathering background information

You need to source and use good quality background information on the topic of your CBA. To do this you should:

☐ Research and use at least three different sources of information

☐ Make sure your information comes from good-quality sources. (Ask yourself if the information comes from a reliable source or if it might be biased in some way. Also consider how old the source of information is and if it is relevant to your particular project.)

☐ Try to check that your information is correct by verifying it against different sources

☐ Use different types of sources

Look at the following types of sources and circle the types of sources you will try to use:

| Newspapers/magazines | Books | Websites | Information leaflets |

| Videos | Photographs | Audio recordings | Libraries | Interviews |

| Surveys | Visits to local information centres | Data sources (e.g. relevant statistics) |

Others: _____

Now pick out your top three sources and describe the useful information you found in each source.

Source 1: _____

Useful information from Source 1:

_____

_____

_____

How do you know this information is reliable?

_____

_____

Source 2: _____

Useful information from Source 2:

_____

_____

_____

How do you know this information is reliable?

_____

_____

Source 3: _____

Useful information from Source 3:

_____

_____

_____

How do you know this information is reliable?

_____

_____

C. Showing creativity and original interpretation

Presentation

Think about other projects and resources you have seen on this topic. How will your presentation of information be different and unique?

- ☐ I will use a **form of presentation** that has never been used before for this topic.
- ☐ I will present the information in a way that is much **more suitable for my target audience**.
- ☐ I will present the information from a **unique viewpoint**.
- ☐ I will use **artistic skills** to present the project in a unique way.
- ☐ Other: _____

Explain how the **presentation** of your project will be unique and show excellent levels of creativity:

_____

_____

Original interpretation of material

What will be original about the content of your project?

- ☐ I will look at the topic from a **local perspective**.
- ☐ I will include **original data** (I will carry out my own surveys, interviews, etc.)
- ☐ I will engage with the topic and provide my **own opinions**.
- ☐ Other: _____

Explain how you will interpret information in an original way:

_____

_____

As you complete your CBA, explain what makes your project on this topic different from other projects on similar topics:

_____

_____

D. Showing awareness of audience

Describe your target audience.

_____

List three things you will do to make your project relevant and interesting to your target audience.

1. _____
2. _____
3. _____

E. Showing evidence of meaningful reflection

When you have finished your project you must complete a reflection on the work you carried out. Your reflection will be taken into account when your project is being assessed.

You must complete an individual reflection, even if you worked with a group on your CBA. Reflections may be completed in oral or written form.

Use the Sample Reflection Template on the next page or the following sentences to help you complete your reflection:

In this project, I was/we were asked to ...

In completing this project, the best sources of information were ... because ...

My particular contribution to the project was ...

By doing this project I learned the following about this topic ...

Completing this project has influenced my thinking/behaviour/attitudes in the following ways: ...

I think that this learning is important for young people because ...

Sample Reflection Template

Strands:_____

Topic: _____

Outline of the project:_____

_____

How I/we completed the project:_____

_____

_____

Important information sourced and how I/we made decisions about what to include:

_____

_____

_____

My role in the project and what I did well:_____

_____

_____

What my group did well:_____

_____

_____

What I might do differently next time:_____

_____

_____

Challenges/obstacles encountered:_____

_____

_____

This project is important for young people because:_____

_____

_____

How would I apply what I have learned in my own life?_____

_____

_____

_____

_____

WHO AM I?

STRAND 1

TOPIC 1
My Rights and the Rights of Others

Class Contract

Learning outcomes: 1.1, 1.9

responsible connected respected aware

By the end of this lesson you will:

↪ have drawn up the ground rules to facilitate a good learning environment

KEYWORD

Contract

Learning environment

In order to work well together in SPHE class, it is important to have ground rules. Ground rules can help create a good learning environment where everyone feels included, safe and respected.

INDIVIDUAL ACTIVITY

Being able to reflect on
my own learning

Let's review the ground rules that helped the SPHE class to work well last year and adjust the contract if necessary.

1. What helped the class run well?

_____

_____

_____

_____

2. What kinds of behaviour are unhelpful in class?

_____

_____

_____

_____

3. What three rules would you put in place to make sure that everyone works well in SPHE?

1. _____

2. _____

3. _____

 GROUP ACTIVITY

Listening and
expressing myself

Learning with others;
Co-operating

Discuss your ideas with the group. Perhaps others in the group have similar or different views. Try to come to an agreement on five ground rules that your group would like to implement. Write the agreed ground rules here.

1. _____

2. _____

3. _____

4. _____

5. _____

Learning with others; Co-operating

CLASS ACTIVITY

Choose a reporter from your group to share your group's ground rules with the rest of the class. The whole class must now agree on a set of ground rules. Remember: this includes the teacher too! Ensure each ground rule begins with an 'I' statement, e.g. 'I will listen when others are speaking'. When agreement has been reached on these ground rules, write them into the contract. Everyone must sign their contract to show that they agree. Perhaps you could design a poster, banner or collage around your ground rules contract to hang on the classroom wall.

CLASS CONTRACT

Signed:

Learning Keepsake

Three things I have learned in this lesson are:

1. _____

2. _____

3. _____

Something that helped me learn in this lesson was:

_____

_____

_____

As a result of this lesson, I will:

_____

_____

_____

MEET THE CHALLENGE
Strand 1 Topic 1
RESEARCHING GLOBAL CONTRACTS

Learning outcome: 1.9

Part 1:

Working in pairs, go online and research the following document:

○ The Universal Declaration of Human Rights (1948)

Then work together to write a short article covering the following points:

○ Who compiled this document?

○ When was it signed?

○ Who signed it?

○ Is Ireland a signatory (that is, a country that has signed up to the agreement)?

○ What changes did the document hope to bring about?

○ Who is the document meant to support?

○ What rights from this document are similar to your class contract?

○ How does this document help protect individual difference and show respect for uniqueness?

Part 2:

When you have covered these points, write another short article suggesting an area of human rights relating to young people that you think needs to be addressed. You might like to research the Convention on the Rights of the Child (1990). Give this article a title, an introductory paragraph introducing your topic and a conclusion summing up your points.

TOPIC 2
Self-Management

LESSON 2

Goal-Setting for Third Year

Learning outcome: 1.5

 responsible

 resilient

 aware

By the end of this lesson you will:

➥ have identified your short-, medium- and long-term goals and ways they can be achieved

KEYWORDS

Goal
Strategy

USEFUL WEBSITE

www.how-to-study.com Provides useful tips on how to set goals and study effectively.

A new school year brings with it the opportunity for a new start, to reflect and make changes. There might be things from Second Year that you are happy with but there might be some things you want to change.

INDIVIDUAL ACTIVITY

Setting and achieving goals

1. In the traffic light below, write down what you want to stop doing this year (red light), what you want to continue doing this year (orange light) and what you want to start doing this year (green light).

Things I want to stop doing

Things I want to continue doing

Things I want to start doing

2. In the crystal ball, write all the things you would like to achieve this year and in the future. Write in as many achievements as you can think of. These can be about your personal life, school life, sports, hobbies, friends and family.

Setting goals

In order to make your hopes a reality, it is important to set goals. Making a plan can help you stay committed and meet your targets. Goal-setting gives you a sense of purpose and motivates you to keep going even when times get tough. A goal without a plan is only a wish.

> **If you want to live a happy life, tie it to a goal, not to people or things.**
> **Albert Einstein**

Our goals can be short-, medium- or long-term. A short-term goal is something you want to achieve in the near future; for example, 'I want to complete all my homework for every class.' Long-term goals take longer to achieve; for example, 'I want to do well in my Junior Cycle.' Medium-term goals come between your short- and long-term goals; for example, 'I want to do well in my summer exams.' Long-term goals can be built upon short- and medium-term goals.

Setting and achieving goals   **Managing my learning**

INDIVIDUAL ACTIVITY

Look again at what you wrote in the crystal ball and identify your short-, medium- and long-term goals.

SHORT-TERM	MEDIUM-TERM	LONG-TERM

SMART goal-setting

One effective approach to setting goals is the **SMART** strategy, which breaks goals into component parts to make them clearer and more specific.

Specific: State exactly what it is you want to achieve and to what extent. A good goal should not be vague; it should be clear and concise and should answer the questions, whether those questions are which, what, who, where, when or why?

> ***Example:*** I want to improve my grade from 70% to 85% in an upcoming maths test. (*This is a smart goal, as it is specific and measurable. It is also time-bound as the test will take place on a given date in the future. We can assume that the goal is also achievable and relevant.*)

Measurable: Goals must be defined in numerical or measurable terms. By recording your actions and improvements, you can track your progress and measure the outcome. This will help to keep you motivated and allow you to set milestones that you can celebrate when you achieve them, or re-evaluate if you don't. A good goal should answer the question, 'How much or how many?'

> ***Example:*** I will complete the last five years of maths exam papers. (*By tracking your progress, you should see an improvement in your work as you achieve more correct answers with each paper.*)

Achievable: Too many people fall into the trap of setting impossible goals. While impossible goals may push you forward for a while, it is likely that you will give up on them at some future point. Goals should be challenging, but achievable. A good goal should describe a result.

> **Example:** I will focus on mastering and answering correctly all the trigonometry and geometry questions in past maths papers.

Relevant: The goal should be relevant to you and your overall plan, otherwise achieving it may be a pointless exercise. To ensure your goal is beneficial, make sure that it is worth your time and will provide positive benefits to you. While goals may appear optimistic initially, as you devise ways of achieving them, they become more realistic.

> **Example:** I will keep a checklist of the papers I need to complete, and will tick them off as I finish each paper. *(You should see improvements in your ability to master the questions as you progress through the list.)*

Time-based: Goals should include a time limit. A good goal should indicate by when and how much time you need to achieve your goal.

> **Example:** I will have reviewed two of the five past maths exam papers by this day week.

INDIVIDUAL ACTIVITY

Setting and achieving goals

Managing my learning

Using the **SMART** strategy, set an academic goal and a personal goal for this year.

	ACADEMIC GOAL	PERSONAL GOAL
Specific		
Measurable		
Achievable		
Relevant		
Time-based		

Tips for staying motivated towards your goal

☞ Sticking to your goal will take commitment.

☞ You will have to check in with your goal regularly to help you keep on track.

☞ If you feel you slip up, don't give up; use it as a learning experience. Everyone slips up, and it takes commitment and effort to stay on track.

☞ Achieving your short-term goals and ticking them off will help you stay motivated towards your bigger, long-term goal.

☞ Use positive self-talk to keep you motivated. Say things to yourself like, 'I can do this', 'I'm not giving up', 'One step at a time, and I will get there.'

☞ Always keep in mind why you set the goal in the first place.

LEARNING KEEPSAKE

Three things I have learned in this lesson are:

1. _____

2. _____

3. _____

Something that helped me learn in this lesson was:

_____

_____

_____

As a result of this lesson, I will:

_____

_____

_____

LESSON 3

Organising My Time for Effective Study

Learning outcome: 1.5

responsible   resilient   aware

By the end of this lesson you will:

➥ have reflected on how to effectively manage your time

➥ have drawn up a personal study timetable

KEYWORDS

Commitments
Timetable

USEFUL WEBSITE

www.how-to-study.com Provides useful tips on how to set goals and study effectively.

Before you can plan to manage your study time, you need to examine how you currently spend your time.

INDIVIDUAL ACTIVITY

Knowing myself

Look at the time-management wheel. Taking the centre as 0 hours and the outer edge as 12 hours, shade or colour in how much time you spend on each activity on an average day. Then answer the questions that follow.

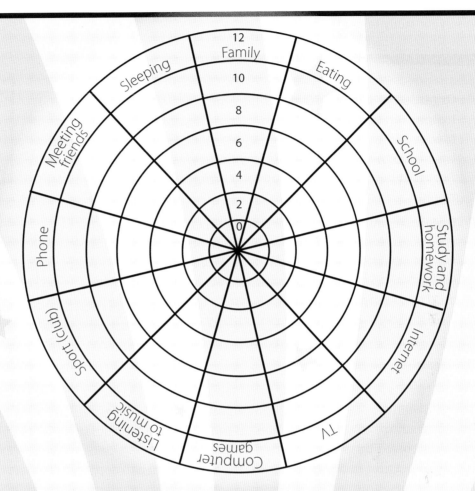

1. What activity, apart from sleeping and attending school, do you spend the most amount of time on each day?

_____

2. What activity do you spend the least amount of time on?

_____

3. Which activity do you like doing best?

_____

4. Which activity would you like to make more time for?

_____

5. Now that you are in Third Year, what changes could you make to how you spend your time?

_____

_____

6. Write down three things you can do to make these changes and improve your time management.

(a) _____

(b) _____

(c) _____

Organising my time for effective study

Being organised is a very important part of effective study. It helps you to stay focused as well as enabling you to make time for the other things in your life. Below are some helpful tips to help you organise your study time effectively.

👉 **Organise your notes.** Organising your notes helps you save time looking for material. Put all your notes and handouts in a ring binder and organise them by subject. At the end of each day, take time to reorganise the handouts you received in classes that day. Do a regular clean-out of your school bag and update your notes weekly.

👉 **Organise your study space.** Having an organised space for study can save you a lot of time. You need a quiet place free from distractions to help you focus. Have a comfortable chair and a desk that is large enough for you to fit your materials on. Try to keep all your materials nearby so you don't have to look for them. Remove any items likely to distract you, such as your mobile phone.

👉 **Organise your time.**

(a) Use a yearly calendar or your school journal to record important dates and deadlines, e.g. school exams, classroom-based assessments, assignments and practical exams. Remember to include extracurricular activities you will be involved in as well as out-of-school activities, e.g. family events, plans with friends, important matches. Keep this in a place you can see it and revisit it regularly to remind yourself.

(b) Use your journal also to mark in the dates you will have school tests, then make a note of when you will start studying for them. Don't leave things until the last minute, as this will only cause you stress. Short periods of study are better than long cramming sessions.

(c) Each Sunday, make a weekly list of what you want to achieve that week.

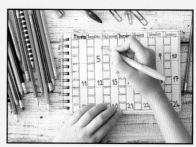

(d) Each night before school, make a to-do list of what you hope to get done the following day. Cross off each activity as you complete it.

👉 **Plan specific times for studying.** Create a study/revision/homework timetable. If you have a set time or times allocated to study, you will find it easier to motivate yourself and achieve your study goals. Setting up a timetable can help you sort out your time management. It gives you a system and routine and makes it easier for you to stick to your plans.

How to create a study timetable

- When you are creating your timetable, make sure to take into account all of your other commitments, e.g. chores, hobbies, even your favourite TV programme.

- Make sure you allow time for homework in your study plan. Look at a typical week's homework and work out how much time you have left for study and revision each day. Bearing in mind your hobbies and other commitments, allocate suitable periods over the weekend for study and revision.

- Do difficult homework first, when you have more energy to tackle it.

- If you get stuck on a problem, try to work it out as best you can but do not spend too much time on it as this will affect the time you have allotted to other subjects. Make a note of it and ask the teacher about it the following day.

- Take regular breaks during study; go for a walk, kick a football, call a friend. Allow a maximum of 15 minutes for each break.

- Be flexible. Remember to review your timetable frequently as changes may occur in your routine.

 ## INDIVIDUAL ACTIVITY

Setting and achieving goals

1. You will now draw up your own weekly study timetable. Before you do, follow these steps.

   (a) Make a list of all your commitments, chores, favourite TV programmes, approximate meal times, etc.

   _____   _____
   _____   _____
   _____   _____
   _____   _____
   _____   _____
   _____   _____

   (b) Identify definite times that you can dedicate to study/project work/assignments.

   _____   _____
   _____   _____

   (c) Write down a list of all your subjects.

   _____   _____
   _____   _____
   _____   _____
   _____   _____

(d) Identify which subjects you need to give more time to.

_____   _____
_____   _____
_____   _____

2. Now draw up a weekly work timetable for yourself. Note that study time does not include homework, it is extra work. Use this example as a guide to help you.

DAY	SUBJECT	TOPIC	CHAPTERS FROM BOOK	TIME
MON	Maths Geography	Trigonometry Rivers	15 10	30 mins 30 mins

DAY	SUBJECT	TOPIC	CHAPTERS FROM BOOK	TIME
MON				
TUE				
WED				
THU				
FRI				
SAT				
SUN				

LEARNING KEEPSAKE

Three things I have learned in this lesson are:

1. _____

2. _____

3. _____

Something that helped me learn in this lesson was:

_____

_____

_____

As a result of this lesson, I will:

_____

_____

_____

LESSON 4
Planning for Effective Study

Learning outcome: 1.5

responsible   resilient   aware

By the end of this lesson you will:

↠ have developed effective study techniques

KEYWORDS

Effective

Motivation

Active learning

INDIVIDUAL ACTIVITY

Reading with understanding

Being able to reflect on my own learning

Read the following information on anabolic steroids as if you were studying it for an exam. Then, on the next page, use some of the techniques you learned in Second Year, e.g. mind maps, flash cards, mnemonics, to help you summarise the material.

ANABOLIC STEROIDS

What are anabolic steroids?

Anabolic steroids are drugs that mimic certain important hormones in the body. The most powerful hormone they imitate is testosterone. Anabolic steroids can be taken in the form of pills, powders or injections.

Why people use anabolic steroids

In recent times, there has been an increased obsession with muscle mass and body image, particularly among young men, and with that a massive increase in the use of anabolic steroids.

People may see steroids as a quick fix to improving strength, muscle mass and sports performance. They also believe that anabolic steroids can help them train harder and recover more quickly.

The effects and risks associated with using anabolic steroids

The misuse of anabolic steroids can have serious psychological and physical side effects. Psychological side effects include paranoia, mood swings, depression and aggression. Physical side effects include severe acne and stunted growth, liver damage, kidney damage and heart failure. Other physical changes for men may include hair loss, enlarged breasts and shrunken testicles. For women, they can cause menstrual problems, increased facial hair and a deepening of the voice. Injecting steroids can cause vein damage, while unclean needles can enable the spread of HIV and other serious infections.

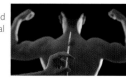

Where do people get them?

Anabolic steroids can be legally prescribed by a doctor to treat certain medical conditions. However, it is illegal to purchase anabolic steroids without a prescription. The steroids that people source online are illegal. There is no way of knowing who made them, or where or how they were manufactured. There is also no guarantee they contain what they say they contain. For this reason, they are extremely dangerous. Consuming these products can result in serious health problems and even death.

Mind map revision

Flash cards revision

Mnemonic revision

The SQ3R technique

SQ3R is a helpful study technique for when you have to read and understand large amounts of text. It stands for:

Survey   **Q**uestion   **R**ead **R**ecite **R**eview

Survey: Read quickly through the text to get a general picture of what it is about. Take note of the title, headings and subheadings to see what the main points are. Look at any captions, pictures, charts, graphs or maps the author has included. Scan the introduction and the conclusion and any summaries provided.

Question: Turn the title, heading and subheadings into questions and write them down. For example: 'The effects and risks associated with using anabolic steroids' could be changed to 'What effects and risks are associated with using anabolic steroids?'

Read: Read through the information more slowly. Read one section at a time to find answers to the questions you raised. Underline and highlight key words and phrases to help you recall the main points. Summarise the main points in the margins as this will make your learning active and effective. Use the techniques you learned in Second Year such as mind maps, flash cards and mnemonics.

SQ3R

Recite: Cover up what you are learning and try to see how much you remember in your own words. You can do this by saying things out loud, writing down key points or getting someone to examine you. Ask yourself, am I answering the questions I raised? If you are still unclear on some points, stop and re-read the material.

Review: Go back over the information regularly to anchor the information in your brain. Remember to use mnemonics and any other visual aid (e.g. sticky notes/posters) you find helpful to assist your review. Looking over your notes regularly is much more effective than doing one large cramming session the night before the exam. 'A little a lot is better than a lot a little.'

Other useful study tips

- ☞ **Organise yourself.** Make a list of the chapters that you need to cover and mark off each one as you revise it.

- ☞ **Prioritise your tasks.** This will help you get started. As you cross off each task, you will feel a sense of achievement.

- ☞ **Break tasks up.** Don't look at everything you have to do, rather break them up into smaller, more manageable chunks. Think about it: how would you eat an elephant? *(You'll find the answer at the bottom of this page.)*

- ☞ **Do past exam papers.** This will help to focus you and prepare you for exams. It will save you time on revising.

- ☞ **Pick a suitable time.** Pick a time that best suits you to study. Some people work better in the morning, some people work better in the evening.

- ☞ **Use visual aids.** Write on sticky notes or make posters and stick them where you will see them regularly, e.g. on your bedroom wall or on the fridge.

- ☞ **Take regular breaks.** Study for short periods, then take a break. You will be more productive this way. During your break, try to get some fresh air if you can.

- ☞ **Join a study group.** This can be helpful in subjects like maths where you can help each other out with difficult problems.

INDIVIDUAL ACTIVITY

Being able to reflect
on my own learning

1. Now pick a topic of your choice from your school subjects and revise it using the SQ3R method.

2. Having examined how to use SQ3R and having read the study tips, write down three things you can do to help you study effectively.

    1. _____

    2. _____

    3. _____

One bite at a time!

Learning Keepsake

Three things I have learned in this lesson are:

1. _____

2. _____

3. _____

Something that helped me learn in this lesson was:

_____

_____

_____

As a result of this lesson, I will:

_____

_____

_____

Coping with Examinations

Learning outcome: 1.5

responsible · resilient · aware

By the end of this lesson you will:

➤ know your strengths and weaknesses in exams
➤ have developed techniques to improve your performance in exams

KEYWORDS

Technique
Examination
Preparation

USEFUL WEBSITE

www.how-to-study.com Provides useful tips on how to set goals and study effectively.

INDIVIDUAL ACTIVITY

Being positive about learning

Reading with understanding

Read the following about a Third-Year student, Mark, and how he handles his Christmas exams, and answer the questions that follow each section.

Before the exam

Mark has just received the timetable for his Christmas exams. The exams will take place over four days. His subjects are Irish, English, Maths, Science, Music, Art, French and CSPE. When he does not have an exam, he must go to the general purpose area for study.

1. Take a look at Mark's exam timetable below and answer the questions that follow.

Year 3 Class Timetable
Monday 9 December–Thursday 12 December

Exams will take place in rooms 8, 27, 28, 41, 48, 56, 66, 68, 73, 78. Class lists and exams will be posted on classroom doors the previous day.

Time	Monday	Tuesday	Wednesday	Thursday
9.00–11.00	Maths	Study English	Study Science	Study French
11.00–11.15	Break	Break	Break	Break
11.15–13.10	Study Option 1	Study CSPE	Music	Study Art
13.10–13.50	Lunch	Lunch	Lunch	Lunch
13.50–15.50	Irish	Study Option 2	Study Option 1	

Option 1	Option 2
Art – Ms Coady	Art – Mr Shortt
Business Studies – Mr Monroe	Business Studies – Ms Cusack
Home Economics – Ms Bourke	Home Economics – Mr Stuart
Wood Technology – Mr Keyes	Wood Technology – Ms Leahy
Technical Graphics – Ms Brazier	Music – Mr Jones

(a) Write three things Mark needs to think about or do when he receives his timetable to ensure that he is well prepared for his exams.

(i) _____

(ii) _____

(iii) _____

(b) What materials does he need to consider having before doing his exams?

_____

_____

_____

(c) What advice would you give Mark to ensure he will perform well in the exams, e.g. food, sleep, study, relaxation?

_____

_____

_____

The night before the first exam

Mark remembers receiving his exam timetable and throwing it in his bag, but on the Sunday night before his first exam, he cannot find it. He rings his friend, Rory, and finds out that he has maths first thing the next morning. Mark then remembers that he lost his calculator a while ago, but decides that he will borrow his sister's for the test. After learning his theorems, Mark decides to take a break and call next door to play a few computer games with his friends, Ciarán and Sarah. When Mark gets home a couple of hours later, he is very tired. He decides that he will get up early the next morning to do a bit more study before school.

What could Mark have done before his exam that would have improved his performance?

_____

_____

_____

The morning of the first exam

On Monday, Mark sleeps late so he doesn't have time to cram the extra study he wanted to. He also doesn't have time to make his lunch because he has to rush to catch the bus. He remembers to ask his sister if he can borrow her calculator, but as it happens, she has a maths exam at the same time so can't give it to him. By the time Mark gets to school, he realises that he hasn't checked what room the exam is in. When Mark eventually finds out where he needs to go, he is late.

What could Mark have done on the morning of his exam that would have improved his performance?

_____

_____

_____

During the first exam

Mark is in such a hurry to start the exam that he doesn't read through the instructions or all the questions and begins with the first question. Midway through answering question 1, he realises that he cannot do a part of it. He reads back over the instructions and realises he could have chosen either question 1 or question 2, and he should have done question 2 instead but now he doesn't have time. Mark begins to get flustered and forgets stuff he definitely did know. By the time he calms down, he doesn't have enough time to finish the final three questions. After the exam, he realises he is very hungry but he only has enough money to buy a small bar of chocolate. He has a study period now, and then his next exam after that.

What could Mark have done during his first exam that would have improved his performance?

_____

_____

_____

The DETER strategy for taking tests

As well as knowing the material for your exam, it is also very important to have a plan in place to help you cope with the exam. The **DETER** strategy can help you do your best on any test. Each letter in **DETER** reminds you what to do.

D = Directions

- Read the test directions very carefully and always follow the instructions on the paper. For example, if the paper says that you must 'attempt all questions', you must try to answer all the questions to stand a chance of getting full marks.

- Ask your teacher to explain anything about the test directions you do not understand.

- Only by following the directions can you achieve a good score on the test.

- If you do not follow the directions, you will not be able to demonstrate what you know.

E = Examine

- Examine the whole test; read through all the questions carefully before you begin. Only by knowing the entire task can you break it down into manageable parts.

T = Time

- Decide how much time you will spend on each question.

- Do not go over this time – once you have spent the allocated time on a question, move on, even if you have not finished. You can come back to it if you have time later on.

- Use the marks allocated to each question as a guide to how much time to spend on each question.

- Spend the most time on the questions that count for the most marks.

- Avoid spending too much time on one question so you have little time for other questions.

E = Easiest

- Answer the questions you find easiest first. If you get stuck on a difficult question early in the test, you might not have time to answer questions you're confident of answering well.

R = Review

- If you have planned your time correctly, you will have time to review your answers and make them as complete and accurate as possible.

- Also make sure to review the test directions to be certain you have answered all questions required.

(Source: adapted from www.howtostudy.com)

Health and wellbeing during exam time

Exams can be stressful. As well as putting in the study hours during exams, it is important to look after your health and wellbeing. You can do this by making sure you have balance in your life.

- ☞ **Eat right.** Make sure you eat a balanced diet. Choose healthy snacks while you are studying. This will help to fuel your brain and help you concentrate better. Don't skip breakfast.

- ☞ **Sleep well.** You should aim for 8–9 hours' sleep per night. Try to wind down before going to bed. Read a book, listen to some music. Leave your phone in the kitchen so that it's not a distraction.

- ☞ **Exercise.** Regular exercise can help reduce stress. Build physical activity into your day: go for a short walk, swim, cycle, or do some other physical activity you enjoy.

- ☞ **Practise breathing techniques.** Take 5–10 minutes out of your day to relax and breathe.

- ☞ **Socialise.** You can't spend all your time studying; you need to make time for having fun. Schedule things you enjoy doing on the weekends or between breaks from study.

This mind map sums up what is important when preparing for exams.

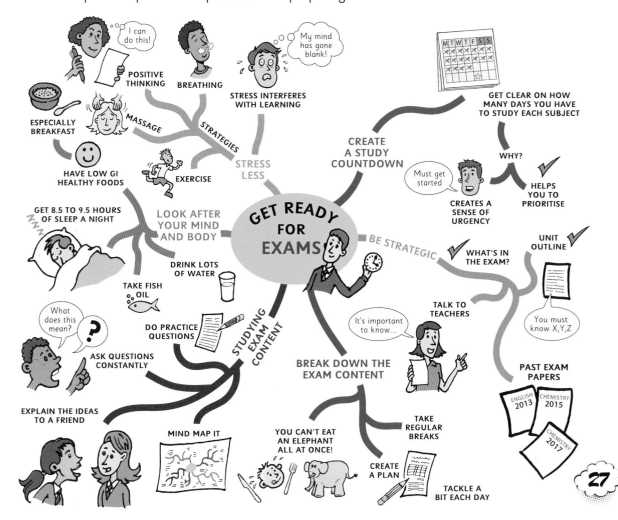

INDIVIDUAL ACTIVITY

Being positive
about learning

1. Write down the things you do well when preparing for and taking exams.

_____
_____
_____
_____

2. Write down areas you could improve on.

_____
_____
_____
_____
_____

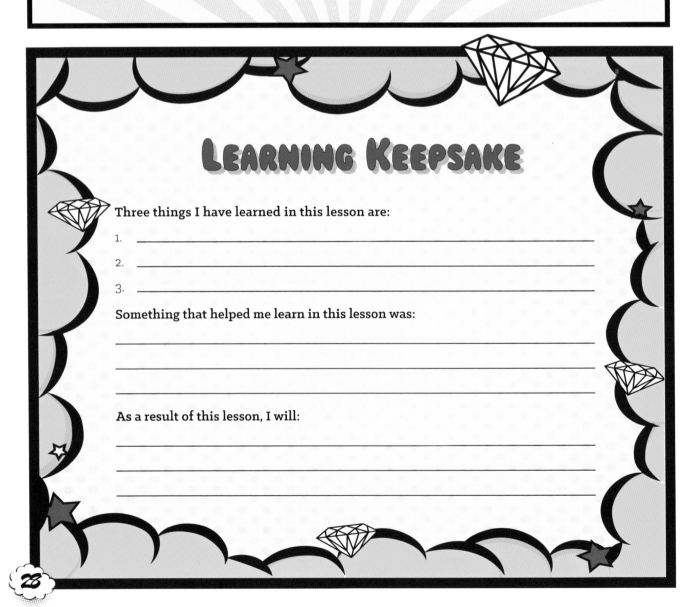

LEARNING KEEPSAKE

Three things I have learned in this lesson are:

1. _____
2. _____
3. _____

Something that helped me learn in this lesson was:

_____
_____
_____

As a result of this lesson, I will:

_____
_____
_____

LESSON 6
Health and Wellbeing Sources of Information

Learning outcome: 1.7

 responsible resilient aware

By the end of this lesson you will:

•▸ be able to identify reliable and appropriate sources of information about health and wellbeing

•▸ understand what makes a website reliable and trustworthy

KEYWORDS

Source	Secure
Reliable	Biased
Appropriate	Accurate

USEFUL WEBSITES

www.hse.ie Provides information on health services available in Ireland.

www.childline.ie A 24-hour helpline and online support service offering advice and support to children and young people under 18. Freephone 1800 666 666.

www.samaritans.ie Provides emotional support for people experiencing despair or distress.

www.spunout.ie/health/article/confidentiality An article about young people's rights regarding medical consent and confidentiality.

From time to time we may seek advice in relation to health and wellbeing. Some sources are more reliable and trustworthy than others, so it is vital that we understand where to find accurate and appropriate information.

INDIVIDUAL ACTIVITY

Thinking critically

Read the following scenarios and decide if the person is using reliable/unreliable sources of information by ticking the relevant box. Then answer the questions that follow each scenario.

	RELIABLE	UNRELIABLE	NOT SURE
Mary is worried: she is struggling to cope with her exams. She goes online and finds an exam advice blog.	☐	☐	☐

Is this a reliable source of information/help? Explain.

_____

_____

_____

Where might Mary go for more reliable/trustworthy advice?

_____

_____

	RELIABLE	UNRELIABLE	NOT SURE
Tom's father is drinking too much, so Tom logs onto an HSE website for advice/support.	☐	☐	☐

Is this a reliable source of information/help? Explain.

_____

_____

_____

Where might Tom go for more reliable/trustworthy advice?

_____

_____

	RELIABLE	UNRELIABLE	NOT SURE
Anne is trying to lose weight. She finds a great diet in a magazine where it says she can lose 10 lb in 10 days.	☐	☐	☐

Is this a reliable source of information/help? Explain.

_____

_____

_____

Where might Anne go for more reliable/trustworthy advice?

_____

_____

Kate has found a lump under her arm. She logs onto an online forum to find out what it could be.

☐ ☐ ☐

Is this a reliable source of information/help? Explain.

_____

_____

_____

Where might Kate go for more reliable/trustworthy advice?

_____

_____

Alex is trying to bulk up. He goes online and discovers a page offering pills to help build muscle mass.

☐ ☐ ☐

Is this a reliable source of information/help? Explain.

_____

_____

_____

Where might Alex go for more reliable/trustworthy advice?

_____

_____

Karen is feeling anxious and has been stressed lately about her home life. She rings a helpline number she saw listed on a school poster.

☐ ☐ ☐

Is this a reliable source of information/help? Explain.

_____

_____

_____

Where might Karen go for more reliable/trustworthy advice?

_____

_____

Sourcing reliable and appropriate information online

The internet can be a great resource. There are millions of websites that offer young people information on health and wellbeing. You can learn about specific diseases and conditions online and you can find plenty of tips on staying healthy. It is worth remembering, however, that not everything we read online is true or reliable.

When looking up a particular issue related to health and wellbeing on the internet (and indeed in relation to any topic that we're seeking to find out more about), it is important to consider the following.

Source: When looking for information or advice online, you must consider the source of the information. Who is the author of the website? Is the information provided by a qualified person in that field, e.g. doctor, health professional? The 'About Us' section will tell you a lot about who runs the website and whether or not it is a legitimate, trustworthy organisation.

Purpose: What is the purpose of the article? Ask yourself who benefits from sharing the information. Is the information being provided for advertising purposes or for educational purposes? Who is the intended audience? If there are a number of advertisements on the site, the website may have been set up to sell a particular service or product, therefore it could be biased (unfairly promoting something over something else).

SPIDER

Information: Is the information up to date and current? Check out when the site was last updated, which is usually available at the bottom of the screen. Reliable health websites will be updated regularly.

Reliable: Is the information on the site true or factual? Can you cross-check the information on other sites? Can you understand the information? See what other sources say. Can you find other sources from other websites that support the claim. Is the information from valid sources, e.g. medical journals?

Educational: Ask yourself: is the author of this website trying to educate me about a particular issue? Is the information detailed and complete or does it merely skim the surface, leaving out the main facts? Does the site appear to be something it is not? Could it be a hoax site?

Domain: By looking at the domain name, url and address of a website, we can get a great deal of information about a site. Look out for 'https' rather than just 'http' as the 's' indicates that a site is secure. You can also look out for the padlock in the address bar, which also indicates site security. Sites ending with .org, .net, .gov or .edu are usually more reliable sources of health information as they have been created by governments, not-for-profit organisations or educational institutes. Sites ending in .com may represent a specific company. These sites can offer useful information, but be aware that the company may have something to gain from you visiting their site (i.e. they may be trying to sell you one of their products as well as offering you advice).

INDIVIDUAL ACTIVITY

Thinking critically

Choose an issue related to health and wellbeing that you are particularly interested in learning more about. Select a website that you have already been provided with during your SPHE programme, or one of your own choice, and evaluate it by answering the following questions.

Issue you chose: _____

Website name: _____

1. Was the information on the site provided in a way that was easy to understand? Why/why not?

_____

_____

2. Did you find the information you were looking for? Give details.

_____

_____

3. When was the website last updated?

_____

4. Who runs the website? Is it a reliable source? How do you know?

_____

_____

5. Did the website seem biased? How can you tell?

_____

_____

6. Would you recommend this site to other young people? Why/why not?

_____

_____

REMEMBER:

It is important not to use the internet as your only source of information and advice on issues related to health and wellbeing. There are other more reliable sources such as:

- your doctor or pharmacist
- health brochures in your local doctor's office, pharmacy or community centre
- telephone helplines, such as ChildLine, the Samaritans or those funded by the Health Service Executive (HSE)
- medical journals or books

ANY HEALTH CONCERNS ARE BEST DISCUSSED WITH A DOCTOR OR HEALTHCARE PROFESSIONAL.

Learning Keepsake

Three things I have learned in this lesson are:

1. _____

2. _____

3. _____

Something that helped me learn in this lesson was:

_____

_____

_____

As a result of this lesson, I will:

_____

_____

_____

LESSON 7

Making Good Decisions

Learning outcome: 1.6

responsible

resilient

aware

By the end of this lesson you will:

- ◆ have further developed your decision-making skills
- ◆ be aware of the importance of thinking ahead and making good decisions in relation to your education and career options

KEYWORDS

Influence

Future

Consequences

Not all decisions have serious consequences, but there are many difficult decisions in life. For example: What subjects should I choose for my Leaving Cert? Should I do Transition Year? Should I do Leaving Certificate Applied or the traditional Leaving Cert? Because some of our decisions can affect our future, it is important to develop good decision-making skills. In this lesson you will apply the **ABCDE** model of decision-making, which you learned in Second Year, to help Joe solve a problem he has regarding his subject choices for the Leaving Certificate.

INDIVIDUAL ACTIVITY

Thinking creatively
and critically

Reading with
understanding

Read all about Joe Murphy and the academic decisions he has to make and then use the ABCDE decision-making model to help point him in the right direction.

Meet Joe Murphy

Joe is in Third Year and he is going straight into Fifth Year after his Junior Cycle. Joe is very sporty, he loves science and he is an excellent guitar player. He has just received his pre-Junior Certificate results and he is very pleased with all his grades. However, Joe has a decision to make. His school is organising timetables for next year and Joe must choose his subjects. Joe is unsure about what he wants to do when he leaves school; however, he is considering a career in sport or business.

Joe's school report – Christmas exam

Subject	Grade	Teacher's comment
English	Higher Merit	Good work – keep it up!
Irish	Merit	Making good progress
Maths	Distinction	Excellent student
History	Merit	Will improve this grade with more work
Geography	Partially Achieved	Talkative in class; needs to concentrate and put in more work
Spanish	Merit	Good worker
Business Studies	Distinction	Excellent student
Science	Distinction	Excellent
Technical Graphics	Partially Achieved	Needs to work harder to bring this grade up
Music	Distinction	Excellent work – well done!

Joe must do English, Irish and maths, but he has to choose four more subjects so that he will have seven subjects for his Leaving Certificate. The following factors could influence Joe's decision:

- Joe loves music. He went to a classical music camp over the summer and really enjoyed it.

- The business studies teacher is Joe's coach. Joe really likes him and heard that he is a great laugh in class.

- Joe loves history but there are two teachers, Mr Caesar and Mr Roman, for Leaving Certificate. Joe has heard that Mr Roman always gets better results. However, Joe will not find out which teacher he will get until after he chooses his subjects.

- His brother studied chemistry and told him not to choose it because it is impossible.

- He heard Spanish is an easy subject to do well in.

- A couple of Joe's friends are choosing technical graphics.

- He has heard it is very hard to get an A in biology.

Now use the ABCDE model for decision-making to help point Joe in the right direction.

A	**Assess the problem**	What decision has to be made?	
B	**Brainstorm the solutions**	List the different options that Joe could choose.	
C	**Consider** the consequences of each decision	What are the consequences of each possible choice for Joe's future?	
D	**Decide and act**	Based on the facts, the options and the consequences of each choice, suggest a list of subjects for Joe.	
E	**Evaluate the consequences**	Explain the pros and cons of the suggested list.	

CLASS DISCUSSION

Discussing/Debating

INDIVIDUAL ACTIVITY

Making considered
decisions

Now that you have helped Joe to decide on his subjects, identify an important decision that you must make about your own future education. Follow the ABCDE decision-making process to help you make up your mind.

A	Assess the problem	What decision has to be made?	
B	Brainstorm the solutions	List the different options that you can choose.	
C	Consider the consequences of each decision	What are the consequences of each possible choice for your future?	
D	Decide and act	Based on the facts, the options and the consequences of each choice, make a decision about what you will do.	
E	Evaluate the consequences	Explain the pros and cons of your decision.	

LEARNING KEEPSAKE

Three things I have learned in this lesson are:

1. _____

2. _____

3. _____

Something that helped me learn in this lesson was:

_____

_____

_____

As a result of this lesson, I will:

_____

_____

_____

 **LESSON 8**

Recognising Unsafe Situations

Learning outcome: 1.6

 responsible   resilient   aware

By the end of this lesson you will:

- be able to recognise potentially dangerous situations
- be able to apply decision-making skills in situations related to personal safety
- have a greater awareness of safety-enhancing behaviours

 **KEYWORDS**

Risk

Safety

USEFUL WEBSITE

www.suzylamplugh.org A website dedicated to helping and supporting people to stay safe in their daily lives.

Personal safety

Now that you are older you have more independence and more responsibility for your own personal safety. It is important to recognise possible unsafe situations when you encounter them. You should avoid getting yourself into situations that you may not be able to deal with.

Learning with others

 **GROUP ACTIVITY**

In groups, brainstorm risky situations a teenager might find themselves in, where their personal safety could be at risk.

RISKY SITUATIONS

INDIVIDUAL ACTIVITY

Being safe

Read the following five scenarios that any teenager might find themselves in. In relation to each scenario, write down what the potential risk is in the situation and what the person could do to protect themselves.

Scenario 1

Suzy is babysitting for the Smiths. The Smiths have told Suzy that they will be home quite late. The telephone rings and it is a man looking for Mr Smith.

1. What is the potential risk? _____

_____

2. What could Suzy do to protect herself? _____

_____

Scenario 2

Seán and his friend George are attending the teenage disco. Seán's mother has arranged to collect them after the disco. They have both been drinking at the disco. Ten minutes before they are due to be collected, Seán notices George sitting on the ground. He is very drunk and incoherent. Seán knows that if his mother sees George in this state, she will know he was drinking too. Seán is tempted to leave George where he is and tell his mother he got a lift with another friend.

1. What is the potential risk? _____

_____

2. What should Seán do? _____

_____

Scenario 3

Paddy recently received an online message from a girl he doesn't know. He began chatting to her and now he is keen to meet up. She has been flirting with him and last night she asked him to send her some sexy pictures of himself. He is not sure, but he doesn't want her to think he is not interested, so he sends her one image.

1. What is the potential risk? _____

_____

2. What could Paddy do to protect himself? _____

_____

Scenario 4

Helen is out drinking in the park with a few friends. A fight breaks out and she decides things are getting out of hand. She has had a few drinks so she doesn't want to ring her parents. Helen decides to walk home. It is dark and she is nervous but she decides it's better than calling her parents.

1. What is the potential risk? _____

_____

2. What could Helen do to protect herself? _____

_____

Scenario 5

Anne has been out at the cinema with her friends. One of her friend's boyfriend picks them up outside the cinema. Anne immediately notices a strong smell of weed in the car. She is extremely unsure about whether or not her friend's boyfriend is fit to drive but decides to get into the car anyway.

1. What is the potential risk? _____

_____

2. What could Anne do to protect herself? _____

_____

Making considered decisions

Thinking creatively and critically

GROUP ACTIVITY

As a group, discuss using the ABCDE decision-making model and then write down what advice you would give to each person to minimise the risks to their personal safety/to help them do the right thing.

ABCDE decision-making	Suzy	Seán	Paddy	Helen	Anne
Assess the problem What decision has to be made?					
Brainstorm the solutions (List the different options you can choose)					
Consider the consequences of each decision					
Decide and act					
Evaluate your decision					

Personal safety tips

You can minimise risks by thinking and acting 'safely'.

☞ If you are home alone, don't invite strangers into your house. Keep doors and windows locked at all times.

☞ Do not answer any unexpected calls to the door, unless you are sure it's someone you trust.

☞ When babysitting, never admit to being on your own in a house.

☞ Never put personal information on a social networking site. This includes saying that you have a free house.

☞ Never give personal details online; you don't really know who you are talking to.

☞ Never send explicit images of yourself to anyone online, via text or social media. Even if you know the person, it could result in serious consequences if the images were to be made public.

☞ Do not carry all your belongings in one bag. Make sure your personal possessions – e.g. keys, phone, wallet – are kept securely.

☞ If wearing headphones, keep the volume down or keep one earbud out so that you can hear what is happening around you.

☞ Keep your money, phone, camera or headphones out of sight. Don't carry valuable things unless you really have to.

☞ Carry a mobile phone to make a call so that you can get help if you need it.

☞ Have your house key ready in your hand before you need it so that you don't have to stand around looking for it.

☞ If you are using public transport, always sit near the driver and avoid waiting or travelling in isolated places.

☞ Make sure that someone knows where you are going and what time you will return.

☞ Walk on busy streets if you are alone and walk with friends at night.

☞ Avoid places where you think that there could be a danger – dark street, parks or alleys.

☞ If you are worried about your personal safety, go to the nearest place where there are people and call the Gardaí.

☞ Make sure you and your friends look after each other, like taking care of each other, walking each other home or having a designated driver to get you safely home.

☞ Only ever accept a lift from a responsible driver. If you have any doubts, be assertive and just say no.

Now add any other safety tips that you can think of from your own experience.

☞ _____

☞ _____

☞ _____

☞ _____

Being safe

INDIVIDUAL ACTIVITY

Answer the following questions by circling the correct answer. Then add up your scores at the end.

1. You have been out with friends. It is late and you are on your way home alone. You should:

    (a) Take any shortcuts you can to get home quicker.

    (b) Take the quietest route because it is safer when there is no one around to cause trouble.

    (c) Take the busiest route home because there is safety in numbers.

2. It is always important to plan how you will get to and from your destination because:

    (a) You can plan to have safe places along the route if you need to check where you're going.

    (b) You won't get lost.

    (c) Both of the above.

3. If your instincts tell you that you are in danger, you should:

    (a) Get out of the situation without delay.

    (b) Wait a little while in case you are imagining it.

    (c) Ignore the feeling: it would be too embarrassing if you were wrong.

4. When waiting for public transport or a lift, you should:

    (a) Wait near other people in a well-lit area.

    (b) Wait in a quiet area where no one will see you or bother you.

    (c) Find a person you like the look of and stand near them.

5. When travelling on a bus at night, you should:

    (a) Never sit near the driver – you might distract them.

    (b) Sit away from other people to avoid any trouble that might arise.

    (c) Sit close to the driver.

6. You are on a train and someone sits next to you. They make you feel distinctly uncomfortable. You should:

    (a) Avoid eye contact and pointedly ignore the person.

    (b) Move to another seat or carriage.

    (c) Text your friend that you are sitting next to a creep.

7. You receive a threatening message on your phone. You should:

    (a) Tell an adult whom you trust.

    (b) Ignore the message and delete it.

    (c) Send a threat back to the other person.

8. You are planning on having a small party with your friends for your birthday. How should you issue invitations to the people whom you would like to be there?

    (a) Send them a text message.

    (b) Put it up on Facebook and set up a WhatsApp group to invite them.

    (c) Tell your friends in person that you're having a party and they're invited.

Now add up your score.

	a	b	c
Q.1	0	0	3
Q.2	1	1	3
Q.3	3	0	0
Q.4	3	0	0
Q.5	0	0	3
Q.6	0	3	0
Q.7	3	0	0
Q.8	0	0	3

If you scored between 0 and 14: You need to improve the steps you take to increase your personal safety.

If you scored between 15 and 20: You are quite safety-conscious, but there is room for improvement.

If you scored between 20 and 24: You are safety aware. Well done!

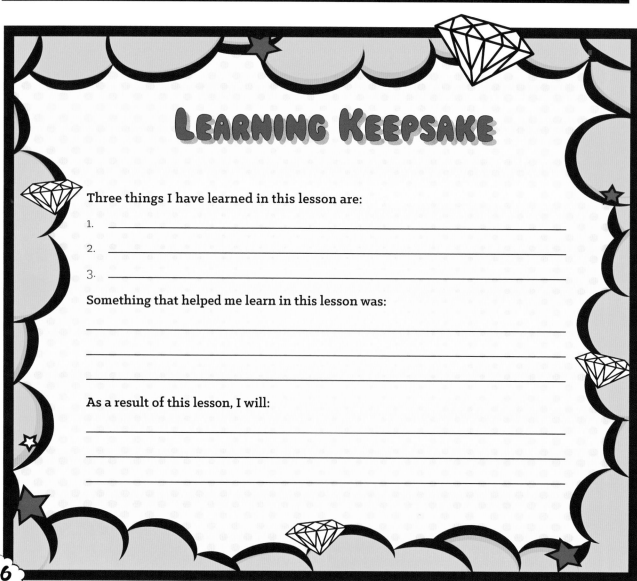

LEARNING KEEPSAKE

Three things I have learned in this lesson are:

1. _____

2. _____

3. _____

Something that helped me learn in this lesson was:

_____

_____

_____

As a result of this lesson, I will:

_____

_____

_____

Violence

LESSON 9

Learning outcome: 1.6

 responsible resilient respected aware

By the end of this lesson you will:
- be conscious of violence as a threat to personal and group safety
- have examined ways of avoiding potentially violent situations
- have developed some skills for handling violent situations

 **KEYWORDS**

Psychological violence

Physical violence

 **USEFUL WEBSITE**

www.suzylamplugh.org A website dedicated to helping and supporting people to stay safe in their daily lives.

Violence

The World Health Organization (WHO) defines violence as the 'intentional use of physical force or power, threatened or actual, against oneself, against another person, or against a group or community, which either results in or has a high likelihood of resulting in injury, death, psychological harm, maldevelopment or deprivation'.

Violence can be psychological or physical.

- Psychological violence includes emotional blackmail, bullying, intimidation and verbal abuse.

- Physical violence includes physical attack and sexual assault.

GROUP ACTIVITY

Learning with others

In groups, brainstorm situations where young people might encounter violent situations.

POTENTIAL VIOLENT SITUATIONS

CLASS DISCUSSION

Discussing/Debating

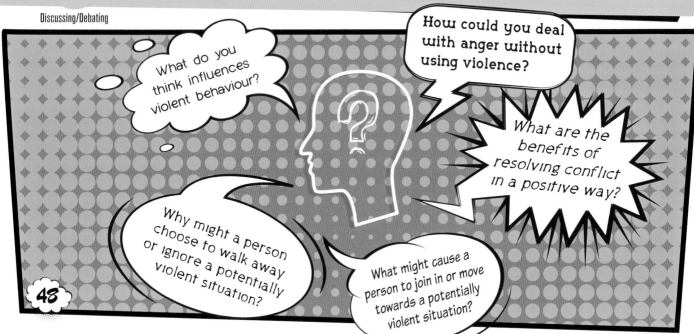

What do you think influences violent behaviour?

How could you deal with anger without using violence?

What are the benefits of resolving conflict in a positive way?

Why might a person choose to walk away or ignore a potentially violent situation?

What might cause a person to join in or move towards a potentially violent situation?

Being safe

INDIVIDUAL ACTIVITY

Read the following two scenarios and think about what you might do if faced with a similar situation.

Scenario 1

You and your friend are up late watching a movie. You fancy getting a late-night takeaway, so you head to the local chipper. You're at the counter giving your order when a group of teenagers barge in and push you out of the way. Your friend starts an argument with one of the group, and before you know it they are asking your friend to 'step outside'.

1. How would you feel in this situation? _____

_____

2. What should you and your friend do? _____

_____

_____

3. What should you and your friend not do/not have done? _____

_____

_____

4. How could a potentially violent situation be avoided? _____

_____

_____

Scenario 2

You are walking down the street with a friend and you notice a man acting strangely. He appears to be talking to himself and seems to be drunk or high. You stare at him as you pass him, sniggering to your friend. Suddenly he begins shouting at you, asking what you're sniggering about. You and your friend begin laughing, and with that he starts to come towards you and threatens to attack you.

1. How would you feel in this situation? _____

_____

2. What should you and your friend do? _____

_____

_____

3. What should you and your friend not do/not have done? _____

_____

_____

4. How could a potentially violent situation be avoided? _____

_____

Avoiding violence

Violence occurs when one or more people have lost control of their emotions. Sometimes it's hard to control our emotions; fear and anger can get the better of us and we can lash out either verbally or physically. Many potentially violent situations can be avoided and it is important that we try to prevent violent situations before they even begin.

Tips for avoiding violent situations

☞ Be alert and recognise potentially violent situations.

☞ Count to 10; breathe deeply and think about your emotions before they get out of control.

☞ Get away – take time out.

☞ Think about the consequences of your actions.

☞ Get help from someone, maybe an adult nearby.

☞ Try to stay calm.

☞ Keep a safe distance at all times.

☞ Do not raise your voice or engage in an argument.

Can you think of other ways to avoid a potentially violent situation?

☞ _____

☞ _____

☞ _____

LEARNING KEEPSAKE

Three things I have learned in this lesson are:

1. _____

2. _____

3. _____

Something that helped me learn in this lesson was:

_____

_____

_____

As a result of this lesson, I will:

_____

_____

_____

MEET THE CHALLENGE

Strand 1 Topic 2

1. WRITE A STUDY ADVICE PAGE

Learning outcomes: 1.5, 4.9

Working on your own, develop a page for your school journal to provide advice to students to prepare and to cope with exam pressure. Your page should include the following:

○ Study tips

○ Time management and study planning

○ Stress busters

○ Any other relevant information you feel is appropriate

Design your page by including a suitable graphic (e.g. draw or find and print an image of a student studying in a suitable study area).

MEET THE CHALLENGE
Strand 1 Topic 2
2. POWERPOINT PRESENTATION ON EFFECTIVE DECISION-MAKING

Learning outcome: 1.6

Working in groups of three or four, create a PowerPoint presentation for other Third-Year students on the **ABCDE Model of Decision-Making**.

○ Try to come up with realistic scenarios where you demonstrate how to use the model. You might decide to focus your PowerPoint around an important upcoming decision such as:

    ○ Subject choice for Fifth Year

    ○ Whether to apply for Transition Year

    ○ Whether to buy an expensive ticket for an upcoming concert

    ○ How to stay safe when out with your friends after dark

○ Present your PowerPoint to your class afterwards in an engaging way. You might use rhetorical questions, a quiz or humour, where appropriate.

○ Consider using pictures, videos, clear headings and diagrams in your presentation.

TOPIC 3
Being an Adolescent

Where Am I Now?

Learning outcomes: 1.3, 1.4

active

responsible

connected

resilient

respected

aware

By the end of this lesson you will:

➦ have reviewed the adolescent stages of human growth and development

KEYWORD

Adolescent

USEFUL WEBSITES

www.kidshealth.org/teen Offers a wide range of advice on issues affecting young people.

www.belongto.org Provides information and support for lesbian, gay, bisexual, transgender and intersex (LGBTQ+) young people in Ireland.

Adolescence

Human development can be roughly divided into three stages: childhood, adolescence and adulthood. Throughout life, people must experience and adapt to many different changes and challenges. Adolescence is generally regarded as a time of great change in a person's life.

INDIVIDUAL ACTIVITY

Knowing myself

Think about what life was like when you were nine years of age and compare it with what life is like now as a teenager. Use the questions in the table as prompts to help you. Then answer the questions that follow based on how you filled in this table.

QUESTION	NINE YEARS OLD	TEENAGER
What are your hobbies?		
What music do you like?		
What is your relationship with your parent(s)/guardian(s) like?		
What responsibilities do you have at home?		
What type of clothes do you wear?		
Where do you and your friends hang out?		
What do you do at break-time and lunch-time?		
Who are your friends?		
Are you interested in your appearance?		
Who do you look up to?		
What mobile phone do you have?		
What social network sites are you on?		
How do you celebrate your birthday?		
How do you feel about school?		

1. Were you surprised by any of the changes that have occurred over the last number of years?

    _____

    _____

2. Do you think your answers will change again in six years' time? Why?

    _____

    _____

3. Which changes have had the biggest effect on your life?

    _____

    _____

4. Do you think that the changes you have experienced are similar to or different from the changes other people your age have experienced?

    _____

    _____

5. What is the best thing about being the age you are now?

    _____

    _____

6. What is the most challenging thing about being the age you are now?

    _____

    _____

The development of adolescents

Throughout adolescence, young people continue to develop and change. Many of these changes are not visible in the same way as the changes that come with puberty. However, these changes are very important as a young person continues to grow towards adulthood and it is important for young people to be aware of them.

Identity

Identity refers to a sense of who we are and how we feel we fit in. Adolescents' identity grows in response to many different influences. Some of these influences are external, e.g. family, friends, the media, etc., and some of them are internal, e.g. our own likes and dislikes. To some extent we can choose our identity, but identities are also formed by environmental forces out of our control such as the country we are born in, the rules and laws we must live by and the opportunities we get in life. Some typical influences include gender, race, class, religion and nationality.

Independence

Adolescence is a time when young people try to be more independent. This can cause them to question their parents' rules and stand up for what they believe is right. Teenagers also tend to

be more influenced by their peer group. As part of their independence, teenagers experiment and take risks. Some of the areas that teenagers like to have increased independence around are:

- how to spend their free time and what hobbies and interests to focus on

- what clothes to wear

- friendships

- privacy and personal space

Values

As a young person grows up, and as they acquire more independence, they become more interested in what they believe in, what they value and what is right for them. They begin to question the values and beliefs that their parents and society accept as normal. Adolescents may rebel and decide differently for themselves. This is an important task for adolescents.

Body image

Body image is how a person views their physical self. It can be influenced by the images we see in the media, where adolescents may compare themselves to images of celebrities and other media figures. In many cases these images have been airbrushed or digitally enhanced and so are not realistic depictions. These unrealistic images can impact negatively on a young person's self-esteem. Teenagers may also find it challenging to cope with the physical changes that occur during adolescence. Not everyone develops at the same time, and young people can begin to question how attractive they are compared to others. Sometimes a young person can also be affected by what their family and their friends say about their appearance, e.g. overemphasis on weight and dieting can have a negative effect on a young person's body image, or overemphasis on how attractive a person is can overstate the importance of attractiveness over all other attributes.

Intellectual development

In the teenage years, young people begin to develop their ability to think abstractly. This means they can manage more challenging information and topics in their school subjects. They become aware of the subjects they like best and they identify their strengths and weaknesses across the different subjects. This awareness is important as it can eventually help young people to think about the types of careers that appeal to them. Teenagers also develop their problem-solving skills and the ability to think more rationally; this can help them to discuss important issues in a more mature and less childish way.

Sexuality

Sexuality is a broad concept and can be a confusing issue for young people. Sexuality is not just about biology, sex or having sex. There are different dimensions to sexuality and these can include:

- gender identity – the sense of being male or female
- gender role – how it is deemed we should behave because we are male or female
- sexual orientation – who we are attracted to romantically and sexually
- sexual reproduction – the act of procreation

Factors that can influence a person's sexuality

- Media: the images depicted by various media can influence what a young person considers normal sexual behaviour.
- Religious beliefs: each major world religion has its own moral code concerning sexuality.
- The laws, attitudes and beliefs in a culture: for example, in some cultures there may be double standards around sexuality; sexual behaviour that is acceptable for young men may not be acceptable for young women.
- Poor body image: this can prevent a person from developing their sexuality in a healthy way.
- Family attitudes: sexuality can be influenced by the messages a person receives growing up.
- Morality: a person's belief about what is right and wrong can influence their sexuality.

INDIVIDUAL ACTIVITY

Knowing myself   Writing for different purposes

1. Look at the headings below and write down the challenges teenagers face in relation to each one.

Getting along with parents	Trying to fit in

Negative peer pressure	Standing up for what you believe to be right

Having freedom	Responsibilities

Relationship pressures	Sexual orientation

Gender roles	Gender identity

Physical changes	Body image

2. Write a letter to your nine-year-old self to keep in your SPHE folder. In the letter, give them advice that will help them cope with the next six years in their life. Include the following information in your letter:

- how much your life has changed since you were nine
- all the positive things about growing up
- some of the challenges that you have faced along the way
- who has supported you and helped you to grow
- who you would go to if you needed support and help with a problem

Dear nine-year-old me,

Learning Keepsake

Three things I have learned in this lesson are:

1. _____

2. _____

3. _____

Something that helped me learn in this lesson was:

_____

_____

_____

As a result of this lesson, I will:

_____

_____

_____

MEET THE CHALLENGE
Strand 1 Topic 3
RESEARCH AND PRESENTATION ON HELP AGENCIES

Learning outcome: 1.7

Working on your own, choose one of the issues raised in Lesson 10 that you are interested in. Research what information and supports are available for young people around your chosen issue. Present your findings to the class in one of the following ways:

- ⃝ Oral presentation
- ⃝ Leaflet or magazine article
- ⃝ Short video presentation
- ⃝ 7-slide PowerPoint presentation

Cover the following areas in your presentation, whichever form you choose:

- ⃝ The name of the agency/agencies
- ⃝ What support they offer
- ⃝ Where they are based
- ⃝ How they can be accessed (email/website address/phone/Freephone/ one-to-one counselling, etc.)

MINDING MYSELF & MINDING OTHERS

TOPIC 1
Respectful Communication

LESSON 11

Learning to Communicate

responsible   connected   resilient   respected   aware

By the end of this lesson you will:
- ➻ be aware of sensitive and appropriate communication

KEYWORDS

Sensitive
Communication

Sometimes in life we face situations that we might find difficult to respond to. We might struggle to know what to say or do. This does not mean that we should simply ignore or avoid the situation. Ignoring a sensitive situation can be hurtful to the person in that difficult situation and can sometimes make that person feel like you don't care. In certain situations, people might find it hard to open up and talk about what is upsetting them. When faced with a difficult or sensitive matter, there are helpful things that we can do or say that may encourage a person to feel more at ease and be more inclined to open up. At the same time, some responses might be unhelpful and might cause a person to shut down and avoid sharing their issue.

Listening and expressing myself

Learning with others

PAIR ACTIVITY

In pairs, read the following scenarios and answer the questions that follow.

Scenario 1

Over the holidays, your friend's grandfather died. Your friend lived with his grandfather, and they were very close. You didn't see him over the holidays. Now that you are back at school, you feel uncomfortable around him because you didn't go to the funeral and haven't yet sympathised with him on his loss.

1. What helpful things could you say or do in this situation?

_____

_____

2. What unhelpful things could you say or do in this situation?

_____

_____

Scenario 2

Your friend is going out with a boy from your class. She calls to your house and is very upset because her boyfriend has broken up with her. You feel relieved because you heard rumours that he has been cheating on her.

1. What helpful things could you say or do in this situation?

_____

_____

2. What unhelpful things could you say or do in this situation?

_____

_____

Scenario 3

Your friend has been fainting a lot at school. You notice that she has lost weight. She often says to other people that she's fat. You have started paying attention to what she is eating. Yesterday she only ate an apple and a yoghurt for lunch. You are concerned for her, but you are not sure how she will react if you say something.

1. What helpful things could you say or do in this situation?

_____

_____

2. What unhelpful things could you say or do in this situation?

_____

_____

Scenario 4

Your friend is very hardworking and always does his best. Sometimes he feels overwhelmed when he is faced with a classroom-based assessment. He gets anxious and lately he has been suffering panic attacks when a classroom-based assessment is due in. You know that there is an assessment due next week and you can see that your friend is already becoming stressed and worried.

1. What helpful things could you say or do in this situation?

_____

_____

2. What unhelpful things could you say or do in this situation?

_____

_____

Scenario 5

Lately you have noticed that a person in your class is struggling to make friends. You have also noticed that some kids often pick on him.

1. What helpful things could you say or do in this situation?

_____

_____

2. What unhelpful things could you say or do in this situation?

_____

_____

Tips for dealing with sensitive situations

- ☞ Don't be afraid to ask a person if they want to talk. They will tell you if they are not ready to talk.

- ☞ Choose the right time. It is very important to choose the right time and place to talk to someone. For example, bringing up a sensitive issue such as grief when the person seems to be having fun is not a good idea.

- ☞ Be sympathetic. Let the person know that you realise it is a difficult situation for them, e.g. say things like, 'It must be difficult for you', or 'Is there anything I can do?' Don't tell them how they should be feeling.

- ☞ Listen. Try not to talk too much. Give the person time to say how they are feeling.

- ☞ Spot the clues. Have they said something in passing that they hope you will ask them about? If someone brings up a sensitive situation, don't just change the subject.

- ☞ Choose the right questions. Choose questions that will encourage them to talk. Ask questions starting with 'How ...', 'What ...', 'Where ...', 'When ...' and 'Why ...', e.g. 'How do you feel about ...?', 'What was it like for you?'

☞ Avoid closed questions. These are questions that only need one-word answers. They are also known as conversation stoppers. Examples include: 'Are you upset?' 'Yes.' 'Do you think you'll tell her?' 'No.'

☞ Use body language. Be relaxed, make eye contact, have appropriate facial expressions.

☞ Don't overreact. If the other person gets upset, stay calm. Don't feel you have to have all the answers – the other person may just want you to listen.

Listening and expressing myself

Learning creatively

In pairs, choose one of the scenarios from the previous activity. Create a role-play for that scenario, where one person responds helpfully, making use of the tips given above. Take turns in each role. While each pair is performing their role-play for the class, answer the following questions in your copy book:

1. How sensitive was the person in dealing with the situation? What makes you say this?
2. Do you think they were helpful in the advice they gave? Give reasons.
3. Is there anything that could have been done differently?

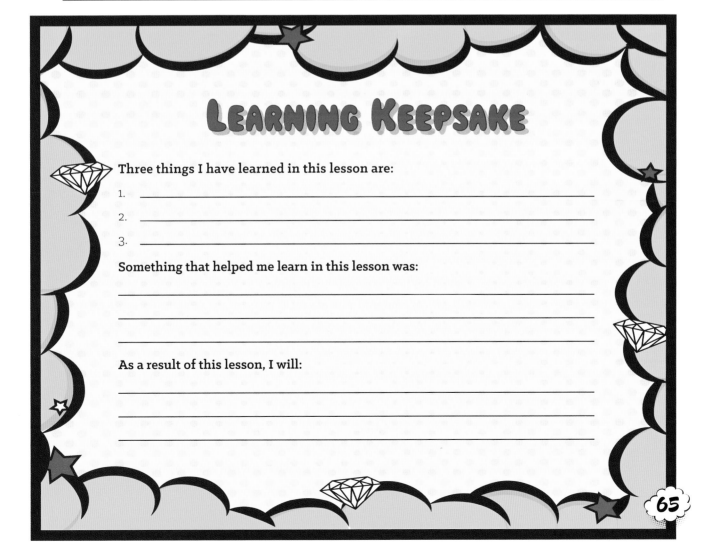

LEARNING KEEPSAKE

Three things I have learned in this lesson are:

1. _____

2. _____

3. _____

Something that helped me learn in this lesson was:

_____

_____

_____

As a result of this lesson, I will:

_____

_____

_____

LESSON 12

Constructive Criticism

Learning outcome: 2.9

responsible connected resilient respected aware

By the end of this lesson you will:

➝ have evaluated the role of constructive criticism in your life

➝ be able to use good communication skills in response to criticism and conflict

KEYWORDS

Feedback

Constructive criticism

Destructive criticism

USEFUL WEBSITE

www.barnardos.ie Offers young people advice on how to deal with many conflict situations.

!!

Throughout our lives we receive feedback in many different ways – we get both compliments and criticism. Constructive criticism is criticism which is well meant and has the goal of improving some area of another person's life or work. A coach might say, 'You're not match-fit – you have good skills, but you need to work on your fitness to make the team.' Destructive criticism has the sole purpose of insulting or hurting the other person, e.g. 'You were absolutely rubbish in the basketball game today.' It is important to be able to give and receive feedback. Learning how to give and receive feedback can help you improve your relationships with others, and it can also help you improve as a person.

Being confident | Listening and expressing myself | Thinking creatively and critically

 INDIVIDUAL ACTIVITY

Read the following scenarios and answer the questions that follow.

Scenario 1

Your mum has arrived back from town with a new jacket she has bought for herself. She loves it, but when you see it on her you think it doesn't suit her.

1. What would you say in this situation?

_____

_____

2. How would you feel saying this?

_____

_____

Scenario 2

You were in your friend's house when you saw him behaving very disrespectfully towards his father. You know his father has not been well recently and you are really shocked by your friend's behaviour.

1. What would you say in this situation?

_____

_____

2. How would you feel saying this?

_____

_____

Scenario 3

Two of your friends, Jack and Kate, have fallen out. Jack is insisting that he has done nothing wrong. You spoke to Kate about it and she told you that Jack said something that really offended her. You want to help but you are afraid to get involved.

1. What would you say in this situation?

_____

_____

2. How would you feel saying this?

_____

_____

Scenario 4

Your friend has always done very well at school, but recently he has started seeing someone, and since then he has started skipping school and generally acting recklessly. You are getting very worried about him and are concerned that he will jeopardise his grades or something more serious for a relationship that likely won't last forever.

1. What would you say in this situation?

_____

_____

2. How would you feel saying this?

_____

_____

The Sandwich Rule for giving constructive feedback

When giving constructive criticism, we can use the 'Sandwich Rule'. This is a way for providing criticism but ensuring that we are acknowledging some positives within the critique we have to make.

STEP 1:
First we give the compliment. This is the bottom slice of the sandwich.

STEP 2:
Then we add the constructive criticism. This is the filling of the sandwich.

STEP 3:
Finally we add the second compliment. This is the top slice of the sandwich.

CLASS DISCUSSION

Discussing/Debating

Why might it be difficult to give constructive criticism?

Why might it be difficult to receive constructive criticism?

Tips for giving constructive criticism

In addition to the Sandwich Rule, the following guidelines are important for delivering constructive criticism.

☛ Choose the right time and place.

☛ Be sensitive to the other person.

☛ Make sure that there aren't a lot of other people present.

☛ Don't raise your voice; speak calmly.

☛ The tone of your voice should indicate that you are trying to help.

☛ Use 'I' statements ('I feel …', 'I think …', etc.), not 'You' statements ('You never …', 'You should …', etc.).

Tips for dealing with constructive criticism

☛ Stay calm.

☛ Listen to the other person's point of view.

☛ Think before responding.

☛ Consider why the person is giving the criticism.

☛ Don't become defensive.

☛ Ask yourself: what can I learn from the criticism?

☛ Respond to the criticism using 'I' statements.

Giving constructive criticism

The following scenarios demonstrate how you might give constructive criticism.

Trouble on the soccer field

Lately, your friend, Anne, is constantly giving out to your other friend, Mary, in soccer training. Anne is extremely competitive and has high expectations. Mary tries her best but she is not as skilled a player as Anne. After training, Mary is upset with Anne's harsh comments, so you decide to talk to Anne.

STEP 1:
Compliment: *Anne, can I talk to you? You know, you are such a strong player, I really admire your commitment to training.*

STEP 2:
Criticism: *Lately I've noticed that you have been a bit hard on Mary. I think it is important that we all work as a team and try to be patient with one another.*

STEP 3:
Compliment: *You are such an important and respected member of the team. I think Mary would really appreciate your encouragement and support.*

The talent show

Your friend, Tom, is entering a talent show and has prepared a comedy routine. He asks your opinion on his act. You watch his act and notice that, while it is good, he is talking too fast and it's hard to understand what he's saying.

STEP 1:

Compliment: *Wow ... Tom, you are so brave to get up there on stage and do that. I really admire your courage – I think you're amazing!*

STEP 2:

Criticism: *Do you think you could just work on slowing down a bit and speaking clearly, just to make sure everyone hears your jokes? I don't mind helping you.*

STEP 3:

Compliment: *Your jokes are so original and I am sure you will be a great hit. I'll be there to cheer you on anyhow!*

Thinking creatively and critically   Knowing myself   Listening and expressing myself

INDIVIDUAL ACTIVITY

1. Read these scenarios and give constructive criticism for each using the Sandwich Rule.

Scenario 1: *Your dad has just started a new cookery class. He hasn't been a great cook up to now but he is starting to improve. The soup he has made you for dinner is much too salty.*

Compliment: _____

Criticism: _____

Compliment: _____

Scenario 2: *Your friend who you sit beside in class is always messing and talking to you. Sometimes it is funny, but other times they get you in trouble. You feel you are falling behind in the subject.*

Compliment: _____

Criticism: _____

Compliment: _____

Scenario 3: *Your teammate is a really good friend of yours and has played beside you in midfield. While they have great skills on the ball, you feel that they are not working hard enough defensively.*

Compliment: _____

Criticism: _____

_____

Compliment: _____

_____

Scenario 4: *You have a very good friend whose behaviour changes when they are in a larger group. They start to show off, slag other people and tell inappropriate jokes.*

Compliment: _____

_____

Criticism: _____

_____

Compliment: _____

_____

Scenario 5: *You are working on a class project. There are four students in your group. Three of you have completed the work required and are waiting for the final piece of the project from your classmate. This student has some fantastic ideas that they share with the group but has not produced any work yet. If you don't complete the project on time, the group will receive a lower grade.*

Compliment: _____

_____

Criticism: _____

_____

Compliment: _____

_____

2. **Think about a situation in your life where it would be beneficial to give constructive feedback.**

   (a) **What would you hope to achieve by giving this feedback?**

   _____

   _____

   _____

   (b) **What would be the best way to deliver this feedback?**

   _____

   _____

   _____

LEARNING KEEPSAKE

Three things I have learned in this lesson are:

1. _____

2. _____

3. _____

Something that helped me learn in this lesson was:

_____

_____

_____

As a result of this lesson, I will:

_____

_____

_____

LESSON 13

Your Style in Conflict

Learning outcome: 2.9

responsible · connected · resilient · respected · aware

By the end of this lesson you will:

- have identified sources of conflict in your life
- recognise how you behave in conflict situations
- be able to evaluate the strengths and weaknesses of how you deal with conflict
- have improved your skills in dealing with conflict

KEYWORDS

Conflict

Resolution

Your parents demand that you clean your room. Someone skips ahead of you in a queue. Your closest friend starts seeing a girl he knows you like. Your teacher unfairly accuses you. A player from the other team insults you during a basketball game. All of these scenarios can lead to conflict.

Learning with others

GROUP ACTIVITY

In groups, brainstorm other examples of when conflict might arise for someone your age.

SOURCES OF CONFLICT

Conflict styles

People respond to conflict in different ways, depending on the situation. For example, you might react one way with you parents and another with your friends. What you are like in public might be very different from what you are like in private. Most of us have our own way of reacting to conflict.

INDIVIDUAL ACTIVITY

Knowing myself

1. Each statement below corresponds to a particular way that people deal with conflict. Beside each statement, give a rating for yourself between 1 and 4.

1 = very unlike me	2 = unlike me	3 = like me	4 = very like me

STATEMENT	SCORE
1. I listen to others and I make sure that everyone is heard.	
2. I usually do what other people expect me to.	
3. I usually argue my point until I get what I want.	
4. I walk away from the situation to avoid tension.	
5. I usually meet people halfway.	
6. I prefer not to hurt people's feelings.	
7. I prefer to stay out of conflict.	
8. I don't back down in arguments.	
9. I usually back down and allow other people to get their own way.	
10. I am always happy to give up something to resolve a problem.	
11. I love a good argument.	
12. I like to listen to everyone's side and then try to solve the problem.	
13. I usually sit down and discuss an issue openly.	
14. If I think my opinion will annoy others, I'll keep it to myself.	
15. In most situations, I think coming to some compromise is better than no compromise at all.	

2. Now add up your score. The fifteen statements correspond to five different ways of dealing with conflict. To find your dominant style, total the points you scored in each category. The one with the highest score is your dominant style.

STYLE		ADD YOUR SCORES FOR THE QUESTIONS	YOUR SCORE
Turtle		4, 7, 14	
Lion		3, 8, 11	
Zebra		5, 10, 15	
Chameleon		2, 6, 9	
Dolphin		1, 12, 13	

Which style/styles are you?

Turtle: You are the avoider. You hate conflict and when faced with any disagreements you do not get involved. Like the turtle, you avoid everything by pulling your head and legs into your shell. 'Leave me out of it! I don't want to get involved!'

Lion: You are the attacker. You are right and everyone else is wrong. You don't listen to or accept anyone else's point of view. Like the lion, you use your roar and your strength to get your way. 'I'm telling you! I know I'm right!'

Zebra: You are the compromiser. You always give up something to help reach an agreement. Whether right or wrong, you always compromise – an admirable strategy; you meet people halfway. Like the zebra, you don't care if you're a black horse with white stripes or a white horse with black stripes. 'Let's split the difference. If you agree to this, I'll agree to that.'

Chameleon: You are the people-pleaser. Giving in and agreeing with others is your preferred style. It's better to be liked than to be truly honest. You believe that keeping a good friend is more important than anything else. Like the chameleon, you change your colour to suit your environment. 'Your friendship means more to me than this. I'll get over it.'

Dolphin: You are Mr/Ms Co-operative. You value everyone's opinion. You listen to the other person's point of view. You are willing to listen and work together for a solution that's best for everyone involved. Like the dolphin, you work with the rest of your group. 'I'm sure if we work together we can figure this out.'

3. Finally, write down the advantages and disadvantages of your style of conflict resolution.

My style of conflict resolution: _____

Advantages: _____

_____

Disadvantages: _____

_____

Changing our conflict styles

The way we deal with conflict varies from situation to situation and from person to person. You may be a lion in one circumstance and a turtle in another. Although we've used the animal analogy, you are not an animal and you have the power to change. Effective conflict resolution requires us to consider each person's viewpoint and feelings.

INDIVIDUAL ACTIVITY

Knowing myself

Think of a time when you were in a conflict situation and answer these questions about it:

1. What was it about?

_____

_____

2. What style did you adopt?

_____

_____

3. If you were in the same situation again, would you do the same thing? Why/why not?

_____

_____

_____

_____

LEARNING KEEPSAKE

Three things I have learned in this lesson are:

1. _____

2. _____

3. _____

Something that helped me learn in this lesson was:

_____

_____

_____

As a result of this lesson, I will:

_____

_____

_____

LESSON 14

Dealing with Conflict

Learning outcome: 2.9

responsible connected resilient respected aware

By the end of this lesson you will:
→ have further developed your conflict resolution skills

Conflict

Resolution

Conflict is a normal part of everyday life. The important question, then, is not so much how we avoid conflict, but rather how we manage it as positively as possible.

PAIR ACTIVITY

Developing good relationships and dealing with conflict

In pairs, look at each of the scenarios depicted and answer the questions that follow each of them.

Scenario 1

What time do you call this?

1. What do you think the conflict is about?

_____

_____

_____

2. Describe how each person could be feeling.

_____

_____

_____

3. What would be a negative response?

_____

_____

4. What needs to happen so that the conflict is resolved and all parties are happy?

_____

Scenario 2

1. What do you think the conflict is about?

_____

_____

2. Describe how each person could be feeling.

_____

_____

3. What would be a negative response?

_____

_____

4. What needs to happen so that the conflict is resolved and all parties are happy?

_____

_____

Scenario 3

1. What do you think the conflict is about?

_____

_____

_____

2. Describe how each person could be feeling.

_____

_____

3. What would be a negative response?

_____

_____

4. What needs to happen so that the conflict is resolved and all parties are happy?

_____

_____

I can't hear myself think!

Scenario 4

1. What do you think the conflict is about?

_____

_____

_____

2. Describe how the person could be feeling.

_____

_____

_____

3. What would be a negative response?

_____

_____

_____

4. What needs to happen so that the conflict is resolved and all parties are happy?

_____

_____

_____

Leave that wretched game alone and do some studying, will you?

Scenario 5

1. What do you think the conflict is about?

_____

_____

_____

2. Describe how each person could be feeling.

_____

_____

_____

3. What would be a negative response?

_____

_____

_____

4. What needs to happen so that the conflict is resolved and all parties are happy?

_____

_____

_____

How to deal with conflict situations

To deal with conflict situations, try following these four steps.

Step 1 Keep calm

- Count to ten.
- Take deep breaths.

Step 2 Deal with the issue

- Choose a suitable time and place to talk.
- Don't raise your voice. Speak calmly.
- Use 'I' statements.
- Keep the conflict between you and the other person or people who are directly involved. Don't ask friends to take sides.

'I' and 'You'

One of the most effective ways of resolving conflict is to use 'I' statements. Often when people engage in conflict they attack and blame the other person, e.g. 'You never want to hang out with me anymore'. This can often lead to the accused person responding in a defensive or aggressive manner. 'I' statements help to tackle conflict in an unthreatening, tactful way. Using 'I' statements correctly will allow you to express how you feel and communicate effectively, minimising the chances of conflict.

Follow this format for using 'I' statements:

I feel _____ when you _____ because _____.

Examples:

You really annoy me because you are always late.	✗
I feel upset when you are late because it makes me feel like you don't value my time.	✓
You never reply to my texts, you don't care about me.	✗
I feel hurt when you don't respond to my texts because it makes me feel like you don't care about me.	✓

INDIVIDUAL ACTIVITY

Thinking creatively
and critically

1. Read the following 'I' statements and rewrite them using the correct approach.

You never help to clean the house.
I feel _____ when you _____ because _____ .

You are always criticising me.
I feel _____ when you _____ because _____ .

2. Write 'I' statements for each of the scenarios below.

Scenario	You have been asked to work in groups for a history project. One of the members of the group is not pulling their weight. You now have to complete their work as you have run out of time to get their work in.
'I' statement	

Scenario	Your friend keeps cancelling plans at the last minute; last week you were all excited about going to the cinema, but for no apparent reason they texted you to say they couldn't make it.
'I' statement	

Scenario	There is a disco on in town every month but your parents won't let you go. You have always been responsible but they still won't let you go. You are beginning to resent them.
'I' statement	

Step 3 Listen

● Listen to each other, take turns and consider the other person's side of the story.

● Don't interrupt or be defensive.

● Try to see where the other person is coming from. Put yourself in their shoes.

Step 4 Work it out

● Talk things through and come to an agreement with which both of you are happy.

● Sometimes you may be unable to reach a satisfactory resolution and it may be necessary to walk away and seek help from a parent, teacher, etc.

Learning creatively

Developing good relationships and resolving conflict

PAIR ACTIVITY

Your teacher will assign you one of the following scenarios. Role-play a conversation in which the two individuals resolve the conflict indicated in your assigned scenario. Use all you have learned about conflict management. At the end, reflect on what was the most difficult aspect of your role-play.

Scenario 1: Friend troubles

You have two really good friends but recently they had a big falling out. Now one of your friends wants you to take their side. You don't feel this is fair.

Scenario 2: Show me the money

Your friend borrowed €30 from you five weeks ago. You have asked him for the money back but he keeps telling you he hasn't got it. You know he started a part-time job two weeks ago.

Scenario 3: Caught out

Your friend is always asking you to cover for her whenever she goes out. Several times she has told her parents that she is staying at your house when in fact she is out drinking with other friends. Last week you met her mother in the shop and you got caught out lying for her.

Scenario 5: Gossip girl

You have been friends with another girl for years. Recently you heard that she has been talking about you behind your back.

Scenario 4: Cracking up

You bought a new iPad which your younger brother is always asking to borrow. He borrowed it the other night without your permission, accidentally dropped it and cracked the screen. He secretly returned it in the hope that you wouldn't know it was him.

Scenario 6: Nit-picking

Your parents are always on your case, telling you to get off your phone, tidy your room, do your homework, study; or giving out to you for coming home late. You are so sick of them nit-picking at everything you do.

Role-play reflection: What was the most difficult aspect of your role-play?

_____

_____

LEARNING KEEPSAKE

Three things I have learned in this lesson are:

1. _____

2. _____

3. _____

Something that helped me learn in this lesson was:

_____

_____

_____

As a result of this lesson, I will:

_____

_____

_____

83

MEET THE CHALLENGE

Strand 2 Topic 1
ROLE-PLAY

Learning outcome: 2.9

In pairs or small groups, devise a conflict scenario that someone your age might have to deal with. When you have devised your scenario, create a dialogue or script that demonstrates a positive resolution to the conflict.

Role-play your dialogue for your class.

Compile a one-page handout suitable for Third Years to insert in their homework journals. This page should give tips on how to deal with conflict in our lives.

TOPIC 2
Being Healthy

Healthy Eating

Learning outcome: 2.1

responsible   aware

By the end of this lesson you will:

↦ evaluate how diet can contribute to self-confidence, self-esteem and wellbeing

KEYWORDS

Mental health

Mood

Serotonin

USEFUL WEBSITES

www.safefood.eu Provides helpful tips and information on nutrition.

www.kidshealth.org Provides helpful tips and information on nutrition.

INDIVIDUAL ACTIVITY

Evaluating information

Read the statements and tick whether you think each is **fact** or **myth**.

STATEMENT	FACT	MYTH
Breads, cereals and potatoes are unhealthy and should be avoided.	☐	☐
Eating late at night can affect your sleep.	☐	☐
One can of fizzy drink can contain eleven spoons of sugar.	☐	☐
Diet fizzy drinks are better than normal fizzy drinks at preventing tooth decay.	☐	☐
Sports and energy drinks are low in sugar.	☐	☐
There is a link between nutrition and mental health.	☐	☐
Chocolate contains caffeine.	☐	☐
The brain uses 20% of all energy needed by the body.	☐	☐
It takes the brain 20 minutes to register that we are full.	☐	☐
Crash diets can make a person gain weight.	☐	☐

We all know that a healthy diet can improve our physical health – it improves heart health, reduces the risks of certain diseases, such as diabetes, blood pressure and certain cancers – but did you know that good nutrition is also essential for our mental health? When it comes to our self-esteem, self-confidence and wellbeing, making healthy food choices can improve our brain function, boost our mood and increase our energy levels. In short, healthy eating habits can result in a healthier, happier you.

INDIVIDUAL ACTIVITY

Evaluating information

The table below outlines the benefits of a healthy balanced diet on our physical health. Write down how each of these benefits could have a knock-on effect on our self-confidence, self-esteem and wellbeing.

PHYSICAL HEALTH BENEFITS	HOW THIS AFFECTS OUR SELF-CONFIDENCE, SELF-ESTEEM AND WELLBEING
Increased energy levels	Having increased energy helps us to take part in the activities we enjoy, which can improve our mood
Improves quality of sleep	
Contributes to healthy skin, hair and nails	
Helps maintain a healthy weight	

Boosts the immune system	
Prevents tooth decay	
Prevents dehydration	
Helps prevent obesity	

Eating for self-confidence, self-esteem and wellbeing

Eat regular meals

Eating regularly and choosing foods that release energy slowly will help to keep our blood sugar levels steady. It is important to eat three meals a day. Missing meals leads to low blood sugar levels and this can result in low mood, poor concentration, irritability and fatigue. If you are hungry between meals, try snacking on healthy options such as fruit or nuts.

Keep hydrated

It is recommended that we drink 8–10 glasses of water per day. Not drinking enough fluids can lead to irritability, poor concentration and reduced mental functioning. Water flushes out toxins, improves skin, sleep patterns, energy levels and can get rid of headaches.

Eat enough protein

Protein contains amino acids which help to regulate our mood and feelings. There is a messenger chemical in the brain called serotonin which improves mood and how we feel. Serotonin is made with the amino acid tryptophan. Sources include lean meat, fish, eggs, cheese, legumes (peas, beans and lentils), soya products, nuts and seeds.

Eat refined carbohydrates

Carbohydrates are broken down into glucose, which is necessary to supply the brain with energy. They give a slow, steady release of energy. This can have a long-lasting effect on our energy levels and mood. They also contain vitamins and minerals such as vitamin B1, folate and zinc, which are associated with control of mood. The brain receives more serotonin when carbohydrate-rich foods are eaten. Sources include wholegrains, fruit and vegetables, beans, nuts and lentils.

Eat foods rich in iron

Iron is needed to form haemoglobin. This acts as a taxi to carry oxygen around the body. Iron helps to stabilise mood and energy levels. A lack of iron can lead to fatigue, lack of concentration and low mood. It can also result in a condition called anaemia. Sources include red meat, poultry, fish, beans and pulses and fortified breakfast cereals.

Eat the right fats

Foods rich in Omega-3 and Omega-6 fatty acids can help our brains to function well. Evidence suggests they can prevent low mood and depression. Sources include oily fish, nuts, poultry, olive and sunflower oils, seeds, avocados, milk, yoghurt, cheese and eggs.

Cut down on caffeine

Coffee, tea, colas and some energy drinks all contain caffeine. Caffeine is a stimulant which boosts energy levels. However, if too much is consumed it can affect a person's energy levels, cause mood swings and disrupt sleep. Caffeine also acts as a diuretic: it encourages the production of urine and so can lead to dehydration. If you take drinks with caffeine, it is advised to limit yourself to 3–4 cups a day or try switching to decaffeinated versions.

Limit your sugar intake

Sometimes when we are not feeling good about ourselves we can reach for sugary foods or drinks to make us feel better, for example sugary drinks, sweets or chocolate. This is often referred to as 'comfort eating'. Eating these foods may give us an initial surge of energy but this soon wears off, leaving us feeling tired and low. Try to replace sugary snacks with more healthy options such as fruit or nuts. Choose water and milk instead of sugary drinks.

Being healthy

Evaluating information

INDIVIDUAL ACTIVITY

Small changes to our diet can make a difference.

Swap this	Swap this	Swap this	Swap this	Swap this
Sugar-coated cereals	Ready meals/fast foods	White bread meat sandwich and large chocolate bar	Battered fish, chips and portion of beans	Crisps (45g bag)

For this	**For this**	**For this**	**For this**	**For this**
Bowl of corn flakes and a glass of orange juice	Medium white roll with breaded chicken	Brown bread meat sandwich, piece of fruit and snack size chocolate bar	Fish fillet, beans, and chips	Crisps (25g bag)

Better still this	**Better still this**	**Better still this**	**Better still this**	**Better still this**
Small bowl of porridge with fresh fruit and a glass of orange juice	Medium white roll with plain chicken fillet and salad	Brown bread meat and salad sandwich, piece of fruit and low fat yoghurt.	Swap chips for wedges and add more veg	Small bowl of pop corn

In the table below, write down any good or bad food habits you may have in each area. Now consider any changes you would like to make.

MEALTIME	GOOD FOOD CHOICES/ HABITS	POOR FOOD HABITS/ CHOICES	CHANGES I WOULD LIKE TO MAKE
Breakfast			
Breaktime			
Lunch			
Dinner			
Snacks			
Drinks			

LEARNING KEEPSAKE

Three things I have learned in this lesson are:

1. _____

2. _____

3. _____

Something that helped me learn in this lesson was:

_____

_____

_____

As a result of this lesson, I will:

_____

_____

_____

LESSON 16 — Food, Media and Advertising

Learning outcome: 2.2

responsible   aware

By the end of this lesson you will:

- be able to critically examine the impact of media and advertising on your food choices
- be able to use nutritional facts and food labelling to make healthy food choices

KEYWORDS

Food labels

Media

Nutritional

USEFUL WEBSITE

www.safefood.eu Provides helpful tips and information on nutrition and food labelling.

Food advertising and the impact of the media

Whether we realise it or not, we are constantly being bombarded with food advertisements, whether on social media, billboards, television, radio, or in newspapers and magazines. These advertisements can influence what we choose to buy, either consciously or unconsciously. Manufacturing companies want to sell their product, so they use a variety of techniques to make the product look attractive or necessary to us.

Thinking creatively
and critically

Below are a number of techniques used by manufacturers to sell products. In groups, try to think of an advertisement you have seen recently that uses this technique.

● **Packaging.** Certain packaging appeals to certain audiences; for example, bright, colourful packaging often featuring cartoon characters is used for children's cereal packaging. Oftentimes, images of food items are digitally enhanced to make them look more appetising.

Advertising/Product: _____

● **Catchy names/slogans/jingles/songs.** These catchy names, slogans, jingles or songs help to keep the product in our memory.

Advertising/Product: _____

● **Celebrity endorsements.** Celebrities are used to recommend and endorse the product by talking about their own experience with the product. The suggestion is that if the celebrity is using it, it must be good.

Advertising/Product: _____

● **Association.** This technique appeals to the needs of the consumer. A product is associated with certain people, activities or places. The suggestion is that if you buy this product, your life will be like that of the person in the advertisement.

Advertising/Product: _____

● **Health claims.** The consumer is promised better health if they use the product.

Advertising/Product: _____

● **Nutritional claims.** A nutritional claim is made about the product. For example, '30% less sugar', 'Low in fat', etc.

Advertising/Product: _____

● **Bandwagon.** This technique tries to convince the consumer that other people are using this product and they should join the crowd. The suggestion is that the consumer will be left out if they do not buy the product.

Advertising/Product: _____

● **Promotions.** There is a promise of getting something for free if you buy the product. For example, coupons, games with prizes, gifts with purchases.

Advertising/Product: _____

● **Facts and statistics.** Facts and statistics are used to make claims about how good the product is, for example, '3 out of 4 doctors would recommend …', 'Scientific tests have shown …'. The advertisement may not give any information about who conducted the test or how many people were surveyed, which means the campaign can be misleading.

Advertising/Product: _____

● **Exaggerated terms.** These are the use of terms that appeal to the consumer such as 'Best', 'Original', 'Amazing', 'Pure', 'Super'. This promotes a positive image of the product in the mind of the consumer.

Advertising/Product: _____

GROUP ACTIVITY

Learning with others

In your group, look at the images and discuss what techniques the advertiser is using to try to persuade you to buy the product.

INDIVIDUAL ACTIVITY

Thinking creatively and critically

A lot of time goes into the packaging of products to make them more appealing to us. The way the product is packaged is a form of advertising. Look at the images of these three cereals and answer the questions in the table.

CEREAL 1

CEREAL 2

CEREAL 3

QUESTIONS	CEREAL 1	CEREAL 2	CEREAL 3
Who is the product targeted at? How can you tell?			
Does the packaging appeal to you?			
Do you think this is a healthy product? Why? What other information might you need?			
What techniques does the manufacturer use to persuade you to buy the product? Are there any health or nutrition claims?			

Food item claims

Nutritional claims

A nutritional claim is any claim that implies that a product has a particular beneficial nutritional property.

| Low fat | No added sugar | High in Vitamin C | High in fibre | Low salt/sodium |

Health claims

A health claim is a claim that states, suggests or implies that the product may in some way improve your health or lifestyle. It may also claim to protect you from disease or illness.

Endorsed nutritional claims

In order to make nutritional claims, the manufacturer must comply with the following guidelines:

'Low in fat' = the product must contain less than 5 g fat per 100 g

'Low in saturates' = the product must contain less than 3 g saturated fat in 100 g

'Virtually fat-free' = the product must contain less than 0.3 g fat in 100 g

'Reduced fat' = the product must contain at least 25% less fat than a standard product

'Low sugar' = the product must contain less than 5 g sugar in 100 g

'No added sugar' = the product must not contain any extra added sugar

'Reduced sugar' = the product must contain at least 25% less sugar than a standard product

'High fibre' = the product must contain at least 6 g fibre in 100 g

'Reduced salt/sodium' = the product must contain at least 25% less sodium (salt) than a standard product

'Low calorie/diet' = the product must contain less than 40 calories in 100 g or 100 ml

(Source: The Irish Nutrition and Dietetic Institute)

It is important that we learn to make healthy choices and that we are not completely led by glamorised packaging/advertising, health or nutritional claims. If a manufacturer is making one of these claims, it may not necessarily mean that the product is healthy; for example, it might be low in fat, but high in sugar. This is why it is important to look more closely at the product's nutritional label. Truly healthy foods are low in fat, low in sugar and high in fibre.

Food labelling

In order to understand what you are eating and to make healthy food choices, you need to be able to make sense of food labels. Under EU law, all pre-packed foods must provide nutrition information. The food nutrition label tells us about the amount of nutrients in the product.

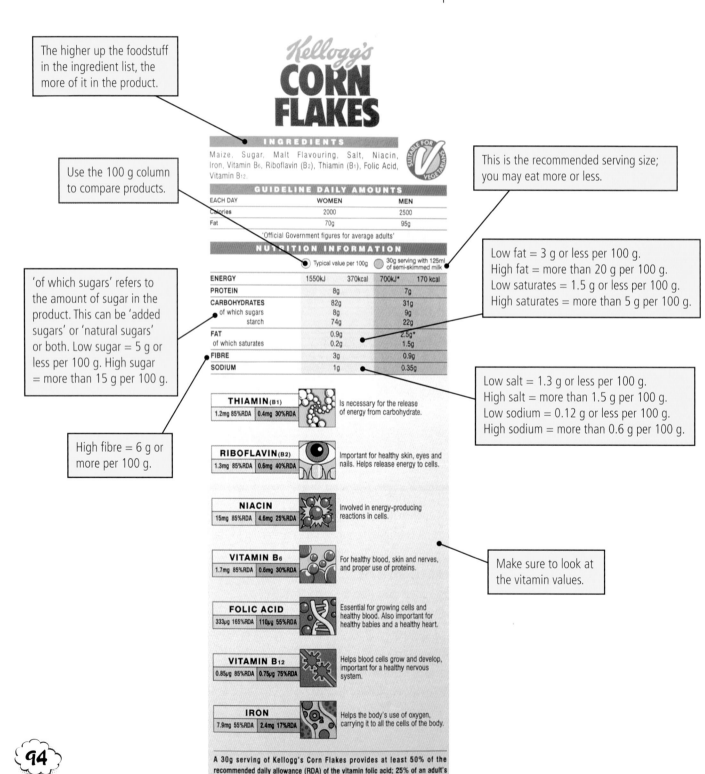

The higher up the foodstuff in the ingredient list, the more of it in the product.

Use the 100 g column to compare products.

This is the recommended serving size; you may eat more or less.

Low fat = 3 g or less per 100 g.
High fat = more than 20 g per 100 g.
Low saturates = 1.5 g or less per 100 g.
High saturates = more than 5 g per 100 g.

'of which sugars' refers to the amount of sugar in the product. This can be 'added sugars' or 'natural sugars' or both. Low sugar = 5 g or less per 100 g. High sugar = more than 15 g per 100 g.

High fibre = 6 g or more per 100 g.

Low salt = 1.3 g or less per 100 g.
High salt = more than 1.5 g per 100 g.
Low sodium = 0.12 g or less per 100 g.
High sodium = more than 0.6 g per 100 g.

Make sure to look at the vitamin values.

Reference intake

The red, amber and green colour coding on the front of food packs help you see at a glance whether a food is high (red), medium (amber) or low (green) in fat, saturated fat, sugar or salt.

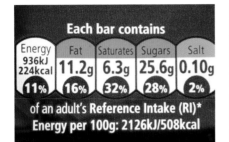

Each bar contains				
Energy 936kJ 224kcal	Fat 11.2g	Saturates 6.3g	Sugars 25.6g	Salt 0.10g
11%	16%	32%	28%	2%

of an adult's Reference Intake (RI)*
Energy per 100g: 2126kJ/508kcal

GREEN means low in that nutrient and indicates a healthier choice

AMBER means there is a medium amount of that nutrient in the serving.

RED means it is high in that nutrient

If you look closely at the packaging, you will see what percentage of your daily reference intakes each portion of that food contains. For example, the food label above shows you that each portion will provide you with 11.2 g of fat, which is 16% of your daily intake for fat.

INDIVIDUAL ACTIVITY

Evaluating information and data

Below are three cereal food labels. Pick one of them to examine and answer the questions.

LABEL 1

Great to know

Nutrition

Typical values	per 100g	per 50g serving	% adult GDA 50g serving no milk
Energy kJ	1399	699	
Energy kcal	331	165	8.3%
Protein	7.4g	3.7g	8.2%
Carbohydrate	71.4g	35.7g	15.5%
of which sugars	19.7g	9.9g	11.0%
of which polyols	6.9g	3.5g	-
of which starch	44.8g	22.4g	-
Fat	1.3g	0.7g	1.0%
of which saturates	0.3g	0.1g	0.5%
Fibre	7.5g	3.8g	15.8%
Salt	0.23g	0.12g	2.0%
of which sodium	0.09g	0.05g	2.1%

	per 50g with 100ml semi-skimmed milk	adult	GDA children (5-10 yrs)
Energy kJ	903		
Energy kcal	214	2000	1800
Protein	7.2g	45g	24g
Carbohydrate	40.7g	230g	220g
of which sugars	14.6g	90g	85g
of which polyols	3.5g	-	-
of which starch	22.4g	-	-
Fat	2.3g	70g	70g
of which saturates	1.2g	20g	20g
Fibre	3.8g	24g	15g
Salt	0.26g	6g	4g
of which sodium	0.10g	2.4g	1.4g

Calories/Fat per serving with whole milk: 232 kcal/4.6g
Calories/Fat per serving with skimmed milk: 201 kcal/1.0g

LABEL 2

Nutrition Facts
Serving Size 1 cup (32g)
Servings Per Container about 9

Amount Per Serving	Trix	with ⅓ cup skim milk
Calories	130	170
Calories from Fat	15	15

	% Daily Value**	
Total Fat 1.5g*	2%	3%
Saturated Fat 0g	0%	0%
Trans Fat 0g		
Polyunsaturated Fat 0.5g		
Monounsaturated Fat 1g		
Cholesterol 0mg	0%	1%
Sodium 160mg	7%	9%
Potassium 50mg	1%	7%
Total Carbohydrate 27g	9%	11%
Dietary Fiber 1g	5%	5%
Sugars 9g		
Other Carbohydrate 17g		
Protein 1g		
Vitamin A	10%	15%
Vitamin C	10%	10%

LABEL 3

Typical Values	Per 100g	Per servin (50g with 125ml semi-skimmed milk)
Energy	1593kJ	1063kJ
	379kcal	252kcal
Protein	8.4g	
Carbohydrate	60.3g	8.6g
of which sugars	24.4g	36.0g
Fat	12.2g	18.1g
of which saturates	1.4g	8.2g
Fibre	9.2g	2.1g
Sodium	0.01g	4.6g
Salt Equivalent	0.02g	0.06g
		0.1g

1. What can you say about the salt, sugar and fat content of the product?

   Sugar: _____

   Salt: _____

   Fat: _____

2. After examining the label, would you choose this product? Is it healthy? Why?

   _____

   _____

LEARNING KEEPSAKE

Three things I have learned in this lesson are:

1. _____

2. _____

3. _____

Something that helped me learn in this lesson was:

_____

_____

_____

As a result of this lesson, I will:

_____

_____

_____

Physical Activity

Learning outcome: 2.1

By the end of this lesson you will:

→ appreciate the need for physical exercise in your life and its contribution to your overall wellbeing

→ have reflected on your current activity levels

→ have planned an exercise programme that suits your life

→ understand how physical activity can contribute to self-esteem, self-confidence and wellbeing

KEYWORDS

Physically active

Recreational activities

Moderate exercise

Vigorous exercise

www.getirelandactive.ie Provides information and advice on how to get active.

INDIVIDUAL ACTIVITY

Knowing myself

Complete the quiz to determine how active you are. For each question, circle the answer that most applies to you.

1. How many days per week would you do 60 minutes of moderate to vigorous activity?

   (a) 5 or more

   (b) 2–4

   (c) 0–1

2. How would you describe your fitness level?

   (a) Very fit

   (b) Quite fit

   (c) Very unfit

3. When you are out and about, do you normally:

    (a) Take the stairs?

    (b) Take the lift and walk?

    (c) Take the lift?

4. Are you physically active at home, e.g. would you walk to the shop, walk the dog, do the vacuuming, mow the lawn:

    (a) A lot of the time

    (b) Sometimes, but only when I have to

    (c) Never

5. During break at school, do you spend most of your time:

    (a) Doing an activity in the playground?

    (b) Walking around the corridors with friends?

    (c) Sitting down talking to friends?

6. How would you describe your participation in PE class?

    (a) I love PE and rarely miss it.

    (b) I like doing it most of the time depending on the activity.

    (c) I usually try to get out of it by forgetting my gear or bringing in a note.

7. How would you describe your attitude to physical activity?

    (a) I enjoy being physically active; it is a big part of my life.

    (b) I don't mind exercise but I find it difficult to fit it into my day.

    (c) I don't like sports or physical activity; I prefer to spend my spare time watching TV, listening to music or playing computer games.

8. When you exercise, how do you feel?

    (a) More or less the same as I do when I'm not exercising.

    (b) My heart rate is faster and I'm slightly out of breath but I can still carry on a conversation.

    (c) My heart rate is very fast and I'm sweating and breathing heavily.

9. How many times per week do you do flexibility, muscle-strengthening and bone-strengthening exercises (e.g. stretches, sit-ups, bicep curls, skipping)?

    (a) 2–3

    (b) 0–1

    (c) Never

10. Do you take part in physical activities in your leisure time (e.g. walking, cycling, dancing, sports)?

    (a) Most days

    (b) Sometimes

    (c) Never

Your score:

If you circled mostly 'a's: Well done! Keep up this level of activity in your daily routine.

If you circled mostly 'b's: You have made a good start. Now try to increase the amount of activity you do each week.

If you circled mostly 'c's: You need to get more active.

Exercise excuses

We all have heard about the benefits of exercise. Being physically active improves our physical health, mental wellbeing and makes us more productive and generally feel better. Despite this, four out of five of us do not get the recommended 60 minutes of physical activity a day. It is easy to make excuses for skipping a work-out or not doing physical activity.

Being healthy and physically active

1. Below are some common exercise excuses. As a group, add other excuses people might use to avoid exercise.

I'm too tired

I'm too overweight

I don't feel well

I don't have time

2. Now pick any five of the exercise excuses and try to come up with an 'excuse zapper' for each.

Exercise excuse 1: _____

Excuse zapper: _____

Exercise excuse 2: _____

Excuse zapper: _____

Exercise excuse 3: _____

Excuse zapper: _____

Exercise excuse 4: _____

Excuse zapper: _____

Exercise excuse 5: _____

Excuse zapper: _____

Seven reasons why exercise makes you happier

We already know that exercise is good for us. It controls weight, makes us stronger and protects us against illness and disease. But did you know that exercise actually makes us happier?

1. It releases endorphins and dopamine into the brain. These are natural chemicals that boost feelings of happiness and pleasure.

2. It makes us less stressed. When you have finished exercising, you feel more relaxed because of the way the body reacts to exercise.

3. It energises us. Even though you might feel too tired to exercise, you more often than not feel energised after exercising.

4. Exercise boosts our confidence. You will notice your body becomes fitter and stronger and this will make you feel good about yourself.

5. It reduces anxiety. Recent studies show that the immediate boost of exercise is followed by longer-term relief from anxiety.

6. Being active on a regular basis has been shown to improve sleeping patterns.

7. It can also give you that pep in the morning that makes you want to get out of bed and do things.

How to get physically active

If you are not normally physically active:

1. Start slowly. Build up to an extra 15–30 minutes of moderate-intensity activity 1–2 days a week.

2. Once you reach this level, aim for 30 minutes of activity on most days of the week. For example, progress from 30 minutes on 2–3 days a week to 30 minutes on 3–4 days a week.

3. As you progress, you will get closer to the goal of 60 minutes or more of moderate to vigorous activity every day.

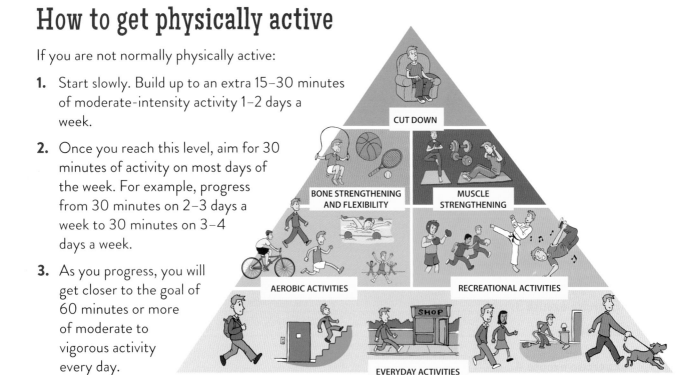

(Source: Get Ireland Active: Promoting Physical Activity in Ireland, HSE)

INDIVIDUAL ACTIVITY

Being healthy and physically active

Using the activity pyramid as a guide, draw up a plan for one week that matches your present level of activity. Ask yourself:

- Why am I exercising? (To keep fit/to train for a specific sport, etc.)
- What time of the day does it suit me best to exercise?
- What types of activity do I like?
- Do I prefer to exercise with friends or alone?
- How will I overcome any obstacles to my exercising?

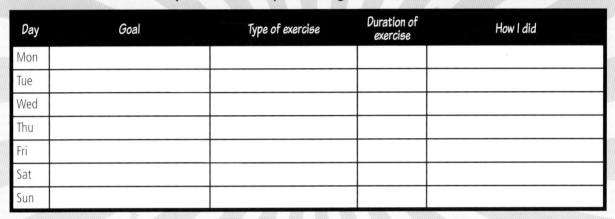

Day	Goal	Type of exercise	Duration of exercise	How I did
Mon				
Tue				
Wed				
Thu				
Fri				
Sat				
Sun				

LEARNING KEEPSAKE

Three things I have learned in this lesson are:

1. _____

2. _____

3. _____

Something that helped me learn in this lesson was:

_____

_____

_____

As a result of this lesson, I will:

_____

_____

_____

LESSON 18

Care-Giving and Care-Receiving

Learning outcome: 2.4

responsible

aware

By the end of this lesson you will:

- understand the meaning of appropriate care-giving and care-receiving
- have reflected on how important it is for young people to be cared for
- have examined the rights of young people
- be able to identify someone to go to if you need help

KEYWORDS

Needs

Rights

USEFUL WEBSITES

www.barnardos.ie/teenhelp Offers support and advice to teenagers experiencing difficulties in their lives.

www.childrensrights.ie Offers information on the rights of children.

www.childline.ie A 24-hour helpline and online support service offering advice and support to children and young people under 18. Freephone 1800 666 666.

www.jigsaw.ie A community-based organisation that offers free one-to-one support to young people experiencing difficulties.

www.teenline.ie A non-profit helpline aimed at young people aged between 13 and 19 years.

REMEMBER:

If anything in this lesson affects or upsets you, make sure to talk to a trusted adult. They can offer you help and support.

All living things need to be cared for. Look at the plant below to see what care it needs to grow.

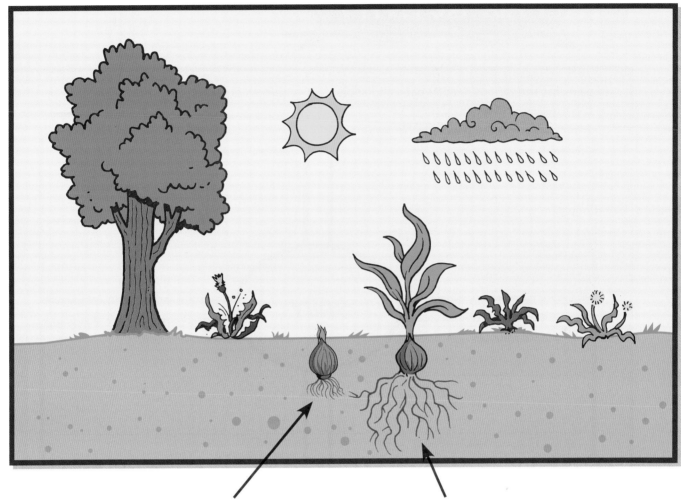

What a planted bulb needs to grow

- Good soil
- Sunshine and water
- Shelter from extreme weather
- Plant food

What a growing bulb needs to grow

- Enough space in garden
- Enough rain
- Enough sun
- Correct temperature
- Other plants growing around it
- Not too many weeds
- Plant food

Care-giving and Care-receiving

Like a plant, children and young people need to be cared for and supported to help them experience safe, fulfilling and happy lives. This support and care is the responsibility of parents, guardians or the state. They are caregivers and the child is the care-receiver. The caregivers protect and meet the needs of children and young people through all stages of their development.

A **need** is something that is required for a person to have a safe, secure and healthy life. This is different to a **want**, which is something a person desires rather than needs. A child's needs will change as they grow and develop.

PAIR ACTIVITY

Learning with others

In pairs, list the various needs a baby and adolescent require in order to:

Survive

_____
_____
_____
_____

Learn and develop

_____
_____
_____

BABY

Feel safe and protected

_____
_____
_____
_____

Be healthy and happy

_____
_____
_____
_____

Survive

_____
_____
_____
_____

Learn and develop

_____
_____
_____

ADOLESCENT

Feel safe and protected

_____
_____
_____
_____

Be healthy and happy

_____
_____
_____
_____

The Rights of the Child

UN Convention on the Rights of the Child, 1989

In order to have their needs met, children have rights. **Rights are entitlements that enable us to live safe, secure and healthy lives.**

The UN Convention on the Rights of the Child (UNCRC) is an international agreement that sets out the rights that all young people under the age of 18 are entitled to. These rights are about ensuring children and young people are respected, protected and cared for. The United Nations agreed this convention in 1989. Ireland signed up to this convention in 1992. By doing so, Ireland made a commitment to work towards making children's rights a reality.

The UN rights are set out in 42 articles – let's look at some of them.

You have the right to:

The UNCRC and the rights can be put into four groups. The circles below shows these groups: Survival, Development, Participation and Protection.

Survival
Every child has the right to have their basic human needs met. These needs are shelter, healthcare, a name and a nationality.

Development
Every child, no matter who they are or where they were born, has the right to reach their full potential. This means they have the right to education and the right to develop their talents and abilities.

Protection
Every child has the right to feel safe and be cared for. The UNCRC recognises that young people in difficult situations need special care.

Participation
Every child has the right to be involved in decisions that are made about them and to express themselves freely.

(source www.itsyourright.ie)

The Children First Act, 2015

The Children First Act was signed into law in November 2015. It states that it is the responsibility of everybody involved with children in an organisation to protect the children's rights and report any concerns that come to their attention to Tusla, the Child and Family Agency, which is responsible for protecting children from harm, or to An Garda Síochána. All organisations providing services to children, e.g. schools, clubs, must have a 'Child Safeguarding' statement. This statement is a written document specifying how the organisation is obliged to keep safe the children they deal with. This document should be on display in a visible place in your school/club, etc.

GROUP ACTIVITY

Learning with others

Answer the following questions:

1. Do you think the UNCRC is important? Why?

_____

_____

_____

_____

_____

2. Whose responsibility is it to ensure children's rights are realised?

_____

_____

_____

_____

_____

3. What do you think are the three most important issues affecting young peoples rights in Ireland today?

1._____

_____

2._____

_____

3._____

_____

INDIVIDUAL ACTIVITY

Being safe

Read through the scenarios below and from what you learned about care-giving and children's rights in today's lesson, tick whether you think the scenario is ok or not ok. Tick the unsure box if you don't really know.

Scenario	Ok	Not ok	Unsure
1. Sal's friend's father gives them a lift to school some mornings. He smokes in the car on the way.			
2. Jake's father doesn't allow him access to any electronic devices after 9 p.m. each evening.			
3. Julia's parents always want to get to know her friends and who she is spending time with.			
4. Carla wants to give up all sports to concentrate on studying for her Junior Cycle. Her parents insist that she keeps playing hockey.			
5. Ben wants to go to third level but his family want him to work in the family business. He doesn't want to disappoint them.			
6. Cian's soccer coach always shouts at him when he makes a mistake on the pitch.			
7. Fran's mother is always checking up on him. She always wants to know where he is going and what time he will be home. Fran thinks she is too strict.			
8. Finoula's parents let her take time off school whenever she likes. She has already missed more than twenty days this year.			
9. Tom's parents work late, so he has to take care of his younger brother. Sometimes he doesn't have time to complete his homework.			
10. Clara's parents don't allow her access to her mobile phone on school days.			
11. All Anthony's friends have mobile phones but his parents refuse to let him have one.			

107

Scenario	Ok	Not ok	Unsure
12. Aaron, who is 15, has to work most evenings in the family pub, which means he starts his homework very late. He is always tired in school.			
13. All Hannah's friends are going to the local disco at the end of each term, but her parents have refused to allow her go.			
14. Nigel's parents know his password to his phone and sometimes read his text messages.			

1. In any of the scenarios above and on the previous page, do you think more information is needed to help you to make your decision? If so, explain why.

_____

_____

_____

_____

_____

_____

2. While you have needs and rights as an adolescent, you should be aware that as you grow in independence you also have responsibilities to your parents/guardians and family, e.g. helping out at home, respecting limits and boundaries. Identify what responsibilities you have within your family.

_____

_____

_____

_____

_____

_____

_____

REMEMBER AGAIN:

If you are concerned about any of the issues discussed in this lesson, you can talk to a trusted adult. They can offer you the help and support you need.

LEARNING KEEPSAKE

Three things I have learned in this lesson are:

1. _____

2. _____

3. _____

Something that helped me to learn in this lesson was:

_____

_____

_____

As a result of this lesson, I will:

_____

_____

_____

_____

MEET THE CHALLENGE

Strand 2 Topic 2

1. PRESENTATION ON DIET AND THE INFLUENCE OF THE MEDIA

Learning outcome: 2.2

Working on your own, pick an advert for a food or drink product that you feel is advertised very effectively. Prepare a presentation (oral or PowerPoint) regarding the influence this product has and the claims that are made. Your presentation should cover the following points:

○ What claims does the advertisement make?

○ What persuasive techniques does it use?

○ Is this product healthy?

○ Who is the target market for this product?

○ How does using this product influence our health and wellbeing?

○ Any other comments you wish to make about the advert.

If doing a PowerPoint presentation, include graphics of your chosen advert/product.

MEET THE CHALLENGE

Strand 2 Topic 2

2. HEALTH PROMOTION CAMPAIGN

Learning outcomes: 1.7, 2.1

Your class has the task of running a four-day health promotion campaign in your school. A different aspect of health will be focused on each day:

> Day 1: Diet
>
> Day 2: Physical activity
>
> Day 3: Sleep/rest
>
> Day 4: Hygiene

Your teacher will divide your class into four groups. Each group will have responsibility for a different day of the campaign and will have to develop their part of the campaign in one of the following ways:

- ○ A presentation (oral for delivery to different classes; written for insertion in school journal; or PowerPoint for delivery in assembly) on your area of the campaign focusing on how your area contributes to self-confidence/self-esteem and wellbeing.
- ○ A whole school-based activity to promote your area, e.g. a healthy cooking display, an exercise class, sleep tips, hand-washing class, etc.
- ○ Posters around the school focusing on your area of the campaign and how it promotes self-confidence/self-esteem and wellbeing.
- ○ Information leaflets on your area of the campaign for distribution around the school.
- ○ Or any other way that your group thinks would be suitable for getting the message out around your area.

TOPIC 3
Substance Use

Substance Use: The Reality

Learning outcomes: 2.5, 2.6, 2.7, 4.7

responsible

connected

resilient

aware

By the end of this lesson you will:

- understand the effects of heroin, cocaine and ecstasy
- recognise how substance use affects mental health
- be aware of how to access information and supports available for young people in relation to substance use
- be able to demonstrate the personal and social skills needed to address pressure to use drugs

KEYWORDS

Heroin

Ecstasy

Cocaine

Psychoactive drugs

USEFUL WEBSITES

www.talktofrank.com Provides information on how to deal with negative peer pressure and what to do in an emergency.

www.easyread.drugabuse.gov Provides information on drugs and their link to mental illness.

Knowing myself

INDIVIDUAL ACTIVITY

1. Read the statements about drugs and drug-taking and tick whether you **agree**, **disagree** or are **unsure.**

STATEMENT	AGREE	DISAGREE	UNSURE
Young people take drugs due to poor parenting.			
Boredom is a factor in drug-taking.			
People take drugs out of curiosity.			
People take drugs because their friends do.			
All drugs should be legalised.			
Taking illegal drugs is no worse than using alcohol or cigarettes.			
There are no long-term effects from taking drugs.			
People who misuse drugs are from poor backgrounds.			
Occasional drug use is OK so long as it doesn't interfere with your daily life.			
Drug users have only themselves to blame for their problems.			
The courts should be more severe on drug dealers.			
Drugs are easy to get hold of.			
Drug misuse is a big problem in our society and it is getting worse.			
If people knew the dangerous effects of drugs, they would not take them.			
Taking drugs to escape problems can make the situation worse.			

2. Using the headings in the table below, write down what you already know about these three drugs. When you are finished, read the information on the next page with your teacher. With a different colour pen, add in the things you didn't already know in your own words.

1. ECSTASY/MDMA

SLANG NAMES	HOW IT IS TAKEN	SHORT-TERM EFFECTS	LONG-TERM EFFECTS

2. COCAINE

SLANG NAMES	HOW IT IS TAKEN	SHORT-TERM EFFECTS	LONG-TERM EFFECTS

3. HEROIN

SLANG NAMES	HOW IT IS TAKEN	SHORT-TERM EFFECTS	LONG-TERM EFFECTS

Ecstasy/MDMA

Slang names: E, yokes, disco biscuits, hug drug, Mitsubishi, XTC, love doves

How it is taken: Ecstasy comes in tablet form and it is ingested orally.

Short-Term Effects: Can start after 20–60 minutes and can last for several hours. Pupils dilate and jaw tightens. Users may feel intense emotions and love for the people around them, enhanced energy and increased alertness. Body temperature, blood pressure and heart rate all increase and users may experience a dry mouth.

Long-Term Effects: May cause anxiety, panic attacks and confusion. As it is a manufactured drug, there is no way of telling exactly what is contained in an ecstasy tablet; other drugs and chemicals that are mixed in can have negative side effects. The come-down from ecstasy can make people feel lethargic and depressed. Long-term users can develop mental health problems. There have been reported cases of death due to ecstasy use. Heat stroke and dehydration are also common risks.

Cocaine

Slang names: Coke, snow, blow, bump, line, rail

How it is taken: White powder that is divided into lines and snorted up the nose. Can also be smoked or injected.

Short-Term Effects: Start quickly and last up to thirty minutes. Users feel wide awake, energetic and more confident. Some people become over-confident, which leads to risk-taking. Heart and pulse rate speed up. The user may appear hyperactive, have dilated pupils and be sweating. They may also experience a dry mouth and loss of appetite. It can also cause the user to feel anxious and panicky.

Long-Term Effects: The user runs an increased risk of death due to overdose as usage can raise the body temperature, cause convulsions, heart attack and heart failure. The risk of overdose is increased if cocaine is mixed with other drugs such as alcohol. Long-term use will cause serious damage to cartilage in the nose (the bone that separates the nostrils). Cocaine use can cause depression, anxiety, paranoia and panic attacks.

Heroin

Slang names: Gear, H, smack, skag, junk, horse, China White

How it is taken: Comes in powder form which ranges in colour from brown to white. Can be injected, sniffed or smoked in a tobacco-based joint.

Short-Term Effects: The effects can start quickly and last for several hours. This can be dependent on the amount of the drug used and how it is taken. It can cause feelings of warmth and relaxation. It slows down breathing and heart rate. High doses can cause drowsiness. The first dose of heroin can bring about dizziness and vomiting.

Long-Term Effects: A highly addictive drug with people becoming quickly hooked. Sharing needles runs the risk of catching or spreading HIV and hepatitis. The euphoric effects are limited to the early stages of using the drug: at first the user takes the drug to feel good, but later they need it to feel normal. The risk of overdose is high as users often do not know the strength or content of the drug. The risk of overdose is particularly high when the user stops using heroin for a while and then starts using it again. Due to the sedative (sleep-inducing) nature of heroin, there is a risk of death due to inhaling vomit.

Drugs and mental health

As detailed above, there are numerous risks associated with drug-taking. One area of risk that is often underestimated is the effect drugs have on a person's mental health. Psychoactive drugs are drugs such as cannabis, alcohol, ecstasy, cocaine and heroin, to name just a few, which affect the mind and mood of the user.

Changes in mood or behaviour from taking drugs is caused by chemical changes in your brain. The substances contained in drugs interfere with the brain's messaging centre and this in turn has an impact on your mental health. This means neurotransmitters (the chemicals that send messages through the brain) cannot properly function, which has a knock-on effect for your mental health.

All psychoactive drugs can cause mental health problems during and after use. These include anxiety, mood swings, depression and psychosis. They may also cause long-term mental health problems such as depression, anxiety disorder, bipolar disorder, schizophrenia and ADHD. It is not clear why this happens to some people and not others. In some cases, using a particular drug triggers an underlying mental illness.

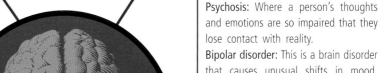

Some drugs such as ecstasy work by increasing levels of serotonin in the brain. Serotonin is a naturally occurring chemical in the brain which regulates mood. Over time, with continued drug use, serotonin levels drop. A lack of serotonin can lead to depression.

Psychosis: Where a person's thoughts and emotions are so impaired that they lose contact with reality.
Bipolar disorder: This is a brain disorder that causes unusual shifts in mood, energy, activity levels and the ability to carry out day-to-day tasks.
Schizophrenia: A mental health diagnosis often used to describe experiences such as disturbances in thoughts, perceptions, emotions and behaviour.
ADHD: Attention deficit hyperactivity disorder, characterised by inattentiveness, hyperactivity and impulsiveness.

Using cannabis has been linked to mental health problems. Research has shown a link between cannabis use and schizophrenia. Using cannabis as a teenager can have long-term effects on mental health as it affects the brain's chemical systems at a time when the brain is still developing.

Sometimes it can be hard to distinguish where drug use issues end and mental health problems begin. Treating mental health issues can be very difficult for this reason. Sometimes people suffering from mental health problems use drugs as a means of escaping from their condition and as a coping mechanism, while others may develop a mental health problem due to their drug-taking. A drug problem can make a mental health problem worse, and if someone is feeling really bad, they may think taking drugs will make it better, which is not the case; it makes things worse.

Help agencies

There is a wide range of drug and alcohol services throughout the country. As well as the websites listed at the start of this lesson, the following agencies offer help and advice on drug use and addiction.

www.services.drugs.ie This website provides you with the National Directory of Drugs and Alcohol services. It enables you to find services in your area.

HSE Drugs and Alcohol Helpline This confidential service has both a Freephone helpline (**1800 459 459**) and an email support service (helpline@hse.ie). This helpline provides support, information, guidance and referral for anyone with a question or concern related to drug and alcohol use and/or HIV and sexual health. During calls/in replying to emails, staff refer to a database of over 400 services nationwide.

Drug use crossword

Across

1. This is a common method used to take heroin. (9)
3. A person can feel this after the effects of ecstasy wear off. (9)
6. This mental illness can be a long-term side effect of drug use. (10)
10. This type of drug is mood-altering. (12)
11. You can acquire this from sharing needles. (3)

Down

2. If a person stops using heroin and starts again after a period of time, this can occur. (8)
4. This naturally occurring chemical helps to regulate mood. (9)
5. Where a person's thoughts and emotions are so impaired that they lose contact with reality. (9)
7. A drug that is common in tablet form. (7)
8. This drug can cause damage to the nose. (7)
9. This drug comes as a brown or white powder. (6)

Learning with others   Knowing myself

GROUP ACTIVITY

Below are a number of skills you have developed in SPHE class. Your teacher will assign you three skills. As a group, write down how this skill could help someone resist the pressure to use drugs or alcohol.

RESISTING PRESSURE TO USE DRUGS/ALCOHOL

Making good decisions helps because …

Building self-esteem and self-confidence helps because …

Building resilience helps because …

Stress management helps because …

Knowing how to deal with peer pressure helps because …

Learning assertiveness helps because …

Having a balanced life helps because …

Maintaining positive mental health helps because …

Dealing with conflict helps because …

LEARNING KEEPSAKE

Three things I have learned in this lesson are:

1. _____

2. _____

3. _____

Something that helped me learn in this lesson was:

_____

_____

_____

As a result of this lesson, I will:

_____

_____

_____

MEET THE CHALLENGE
Strand 2 Topic 3
A TALK ON UNDERAGE DRINKING

Learning outcome: 2.6

As a class, invite a member from your local Garda station or a representative from a local help agency which deals with substance misuse and addiction to give a talk to your class/year group about substance misuse and the types of problems they encounter.

Before the talk:

○ Check with your principal before arranging the talk that they are happy for it to occur.

○ Work with your teacher to come up with a suitable date, time and place for the talk.

○ Collect a set of questions from your class/year to ask the Garda/representative. Your questions could be about the personal, social and legal consequences of drug misuse.

○ Nominate a student who will open the talk and welcome the Garda/representative.

○ Nominate students who will ask the Garda/representative questions.

On the day of the talk:

○ Welcome the Garda/representative when they arrive at the school.

○ Leave enough time at the end of the talk for any questions that might arise over the course of the talk.

○ Thank the Garda/representative at the end of the talk.

TEAM UP

STRAND 3

TOPIC 1
Having a Friend and Being a Friend

Boyfriends and Girlfriends

Learning outcome: 3.3

responsible

connected

aware

By the end of this lesson you will:

↠ have explored the impact of gender roles on friendships

↠ recognise the values of having friendships with males and females

KEYWORDS

Gender roles

Stereotyping

Friendship is very important in our lives. With our friends we can have fun, we can talk about our lives and we can get support. It is healthy to have friendships with people of both sexes. Even though we might think that males and females have specific and different qualities, it is very important not to hold inaccurate and limiting stereotypical views of people.

GROUP ACTIVITY

Thinking critically

As a group, read and discuss the statements about having boys and girls as friends and then tick whether you think they are **true, false** or **sometimes true**.

Statement	True	False	Sometimes true
Boys and girls can't be 'just good friends'.	☐	☐	☐
Boys and girls can't really be friends because their interests are too different.	☐	☐	☐
Boys and girls can be friends if they share the same interests.	☐	☐	☐
Girls are good friends because they know how to be sincere.	☐	☐	☐
Boys are good friends because they know how to have fun.	☐	☐	☐
Boys are immature and it is hard to have meaningful conversations with them.	☐	☐	☐
Girls are gossipy and like to cause drama.	☐	☐	☐
There is no difference between boys and girls as friends. Friends are friends.	☐	☐	☐
Boys prefer male company, girls prefer female company.	☐	☐	☐
Boys are good to hang out with on their own, but when they are with their friends they just mess and act silly.	☐	☐	☐
Girls are good to hang out with on their own, but when they are with their friends they just mess and act silly.	☐	☐	☐
Having boy and girl friends is great because you can get different perspectives on things.	☐	☐	☐
Girls' friendships are based on having conversations, boys' friendships are based on doing activities together.	☐	☐	☐

Why teenage friendships are important

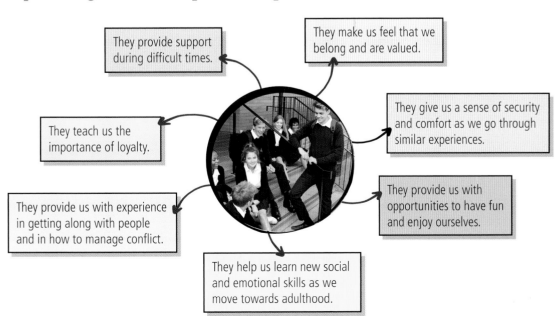

They provide support during difficult times.

They make us feel that we belong and are valued.

They teach us the importance of loyalty.

They give us a sense of security and comfort as we go through similar experiences.

They provide us with experience in getting along with people and in how to manage conflict.

They provide us with opportunities to have fun and enjoy ourselves.

They help us learn new social and emotional skills as we move towards adulthood.

121

GROUP ACTIVITY

Thinking critically

As a group, discuss and then write in five advantages of having boys as friends and five advantages of having girls as friends.

ADVANTAGES OF FRIENDS WHO ARE BOYS

ADVANTAGES OF FRIENDS WHO ARE GIRLS

CLASS DISCUSSION

Discussing/Debating

> Do you think friendship with a boy differs from friendship with a girl?

> Do you think it is important to have both male and female friends? Why/why not?

> Do the qualities that boys value in friendship differ from the qualities that girls value?

> Is there a difference between a friendship and a relationship with a boy/girl? Why do you think this?

> What do you think is the effect of making generalised statements about how males and females act in friendships or relationships?

INDIVIDUAL ACTIVITY

Knowing myself

Think of all the people in your life, both male and female, who you would consider to be friends. In the speech bubbles below, write in all the qualities you value in a friendship.

123

LEARNING KEEPSAKE

Three things I have learned in this lesson are:

1. _____
2. _____
3. _____

Something that helped me learn in this lesson was:

_____

_____

_____

As a result of this lesson, I will:

_____

_____

_____

TOPIC 2
The Relationship Spectrum

Relationships: What's Important?

Learning outcomes: 3.4, 3.5

responsible

aware

resilient

By the end of this lesson you will:

➡ have identified the qualities that are most important to you in a relationship

KEYWORD

Qualities

USEFUL WEBSITE

www.b4udecide.ie Provides helpful information and tips on how young people can make healthy, responsible decisions about relationships and sexual health.

It is important to know the qualities that are most important to you in a relationship. This will help you to make a good decision when choosing a boyfriend or girlfriend.

Knowing myself

INDIVIDUAL ACTIVITY

In the labels, write down the top ten qualities or characteristics that you would look for or value in a romantic relationship, with 1 being the most important to you and 10 being the least important to you. (You will see some qualities/characteristics listed below. You can use these or you can come up with your own, or you can use a mixture of both.)

Loyal	Open
Good-looking	Easy-going
Generous	Shared interests
Trustworthy	Good-natured
Funny	Caring
Intelligent	Supportive
Sincere	Rich
Kind	Dependable
Fashionable	Good listener
Patient	Spontaneous
Adventurous	Driven

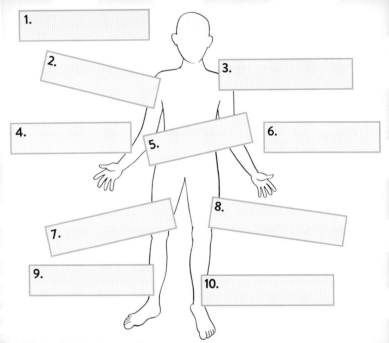

1.
2.
3.
4.
5.
6.
7.
8.
9.
10.

Co-operating

GROUP ACTIVITY

Now, as a group, discuss the qualities/characteristics you chose and decide on ten definitive qualities/characteristics that are important for someone to have if you wish to date them, again with 1 being the most important and 10 being the least important.

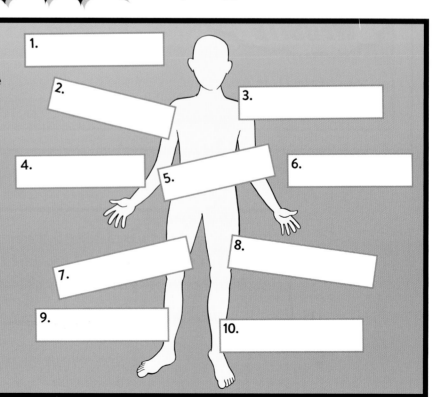

1.
2.
3.
4.
5.
6.
7.
8.
9.
10.

CLASS DISCUSSION

Discussing/Debating

Why do you think it is important to identify the qualities you are looking for in a relationship?

Is there anyone whose individual list is very different from their group list?

Do you think that boys and girls look for different things in a relationship?

Are there any similarities in the qualities/characteristics you admire in yourself and those you admire in people you look up to and respect?

What/who do you think influences the qualities/characteristics a person considers to be important?

INDIVIDUAL ACTIVITY

Knowing myself

Writing for different purposes

1. Read the following starter statements related to being in a relationship, and once you have considered them, finish them in the spaces provided.

   1. Although it is possible to be in a relationship with somebody who has different qualities from you, if two people in a relationship value different things it may lead to difficulties because: _____

   _____

   _____

   2. Difficulties in a relationship can be overcome if: _____

   _____

   _____

   3. Difficulties in a relationship may not be resolved if: _____

   _____

   _____

4. The types of relationship we see in the media are not always good examples because:

_____
_____
_____
_____

5. It is important that the people we are in relationships with have qualities that we value because: _____

_____
_____
_____

2. Now read the following poem, and using the qualities you value in a romantic relationship, write your own poem.

I Will Fall For Someone Who

Is kind to me,
Picks me up when I am down,
Is my best friend,
Keeps surprising me,
Helps me face my fears,
Isn't afraid to say sorry,
Respects me,
Watches movies with me on lazy days,
Knows the real me and …
Loves me anyway.

I Will Fall For Someone Who

_____
_____
_____
_____
_____
_____
_____
_____
_____
_____

3. Finally, write down three qualities you have to offer in a relationship:

Quality 1: _____

Quality 2: _____

Quality 3: _____

LEARNING KEEPSAKE

Three things I have learned in this lesson are:

1. _____

2. _____

3. _____

Something that helped me learn in this lesson was:

_____

_____

_____

As a result of this lesson, I will:

_____

_____

_____

LESSON 22

Healthy vs Unhealthy Relationships

Learning outcomes: 3.1, 3.5

 responsible
 resilient
 connected
 aware

By the end of this lesson you will:

•➤ recognise behaviours associated with healthy and unhealthy relationships

•➤ have explored why people stay in unhealthy relationships

•➤ have identified what a person can do if they find themselves in an unhealthy relationship

KEYWORDS

Healthy behaviours

Unhealthy behaviours

USEFUL WEBSITES

www.b4udecide.ie Provides helpful information and tips on how young people can make healthy, responsible decisions about relationships and sexual health, as well as videos from young people talking about relationships.

www.belongto.org Provides information and support for lesbian, gay, bisexual, transgender and intersex (LGBTQ+) young people in Ireland.

www.kidshealth.org Provides information and advice on managing romantic relationships.

People in healthy relationships experience respect, trust and good communication. They enjoy spending time with the other person and they know that each person needs their own space and privacy. It can sometimes be difficult, however, when in a romantic relationship to recognise when we are not being treated well, especially if we have strong feelings for the other person.

Learning with others

Thinking critically

GROUP ACTIVITY

From this list of twenty statements, decide as a group which statements are characteristic of a healthy relationship and which are characteristic of an unhealthy relationship. Write the number of the healthy statements in the whole heart on the next page, and the numbers of the unhealthy statements in the broken heart.

1. I spend most of my free time with my girlfriend and I don't get to spend much time with my other friends anymore.

2. If something is bothering either of us, we always tell the other person.

3. I enjoy the time I spend with my boyfriend. I feel very comfortable in his company and I feel I can say anything to him and I won't be embarrassed.

5. I usually keep my feelings to myself – I don't think I can be honest about how I really feel in case he calls it off.

6. We both have common interests and we decide together what to do in our spare time.

4. My girlfriend says that if I ended this relationship, she might do something I'd regret.

10. My girlfriend pressurises me to do things I'm not comfortable with.

8. I don't think it is OK if my girlfriend wants to spend time with her friends and not invite me.

9. I don't know where I stand with my boyfriend – I am always worried he is going to call it off.

7. My girlfriend hasn't added me on Instagram even though we've been going out for two months.

11. My boyfriend gets upset when I tell him 'No'.

12. My boyfriend ignores me at school when he is with his friends. He only ever wants to meet me alone.

15. My girlfriend is very loving towards me, and always makes me feel good about myself.

14. My girlfriend calls me multiple times a day and gets upset if I don't pick up.

13. My boyfriend and I spend time together but we also make time for our friends.

18. My boyfriend keeps asking me to send nude pictures, even though I've told him many times that I don't want to.

16. My boyfriend sometimes reads my text messages if I leave the room.

17. We have arguments, but we usually talk them through and we feel better afterwards.

20. My girlfriend sometimes puts me down and tells me I'm stupid.

19. My boyfriend makes me feel good about myself. He often tells me how much he likes me.

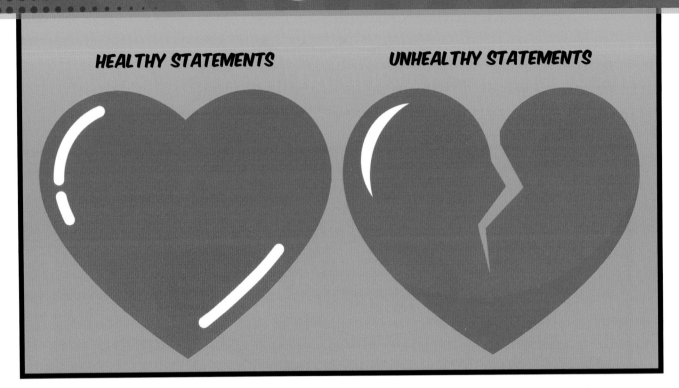

HEALTHY STATEMENTS   **UNHEALTHY STATEMENTS**

INDIVIDUAL ACTIVITY

Thinking critically

Read the following story about Denise's relationship with Luke and then answer the questions that follow.

DENISE AND LUKE

Luke and I were introduced to each other through mutual friends. At first, I was not very interested in Luke but when I got to know him I found myself increasingly attracted to him. We started meeting each other a few weeks later. It was all great at first. We got along very well, we shared common interests and loved spending time together.

As time passes, I have noticed subtle changes in Luke's behaviour. He is becoming more possessive and strange. On two occasions when I left the room, I returned to find him looking at messages on my phone. On a number of occasions, Luke has made nasty comments about my family. If we have a disagreement, he always blames me. Sometimes when we argue he makes insulting comments about my appearance.

Most of the time, when Luke cools off, he apologises to me for his behaviour. He tells me I am the most important person in his life and he is sorry for being so horrible. When I told him I couldn't put up with his behaviour anymore, he said he cannot imagine being without me.

The relationship is not always bad, and we do have good times, but I make an effort not to do or say anything that might upset him in case he gets angry. On one occasion after a night out with friends, I argued with Luke because he spoke to his ex-girlfriend for a long time. Luke got so angry with me that he lost his temper and pushed me. He apologised straight away, and it was the first time he has ever done something like this.

I don't know what to do, but I think I will probably give Luke a second chance because I feel I am partly to blame because I provoked him.

1. How do you think Denise feels?

   _____

   _____

2. How do you think Luke feels?

   _____

   _____

3. Identify four signs that this relationship is unhealthy.

   Sign 1: _____   Sign 2: _____

   Sign 3: _____   Sign 4: _____

4. Who could Denise go to for advice?

   _____

   _____

5. Why might Denise find it difficult to walk away?

   _____

   _____

6. What would you advise Denise to do?

   _____

   _____

What makes a healthy relationship

Here are some of the values and qualities on which a healthy relationship is built.

Trust and support
- Wanting the best for the other person
- Never being disloyal
- Believing in each other
- Offering encouragement when needed
- Overcoming jealousy

Honesty and responsibility
- Being truthful
- Accepting when you are wrong and being able to say it
- Being able to communicate openly and express feelings

Safety

- Never using violence, force or coercion
- Feelings of safety when expressing opinions/beliefs
- Never using control, manipulation or intimidation

Equality

- Sharing decisions and responsibilities
- Having roles that are fair and equal
- Respecting each other's goals

Respect

- Treating each other like they want to be treated themselves
- Valuing each other's opinions
- Non-judgemental listening

Intimacy

- Respecting each other's limits with intimacy
- Respecting 'No'
- Caring about each other's feelings

When to leave

In all types of relationship, there will be disagreements and conflicts of interest. These alone do not mean that the relationship is unhealthy. If there is good, open communication, many problems can be worked on and resolved. If there is something in particular a person is unhappy about or wants to change in their relationship, they need to communicate how they are feeling with the other person, or with a person they trust for advice. A good friend or family member will help you get an outsider's view on your relationship.

However, should someone break any of the above indicators of a healthy relationship, it is important to remember that you are not responsible for their feelings or actions. In a situation where communication breaks down or a person's personal safety is at risk, the person has no choice but to leave the relationship. There are some types of behaviour that should never be tolerated. If you are in a relationship that is damaging to your sense of self or that is violent, you need to get out of it. Talk to someone you trust, a friend, a parent, an adult or a school counsellor.

Even if you are not in a relationship, it is important that you know what you want from a relationship and to be clear about how you feel you should be treated and how you should treat the other person. You must be very clear about and know what it is you will not accept in a relationship.

Knowing myself   Being safe

INDIVIDUAL ACTIVITY

You are now going to write your relationship pledge. When writing your pledge, think about what you want from a relationship, how you will behave and what you will offer in a relationship. For example: 'I pledge to always be treated with respect', 'I pledge to have activities and friends apart from my boyfriend/girlfriend', 'I pledge to treat my boyfriend/girlfriend with respect'.

MY DATING PLEDGE

I pledge _____

I pledge _____

I pledge _____

I pledge _____

I pledge _____

I pledge _____

I pledge _____

I pledge _____

LEARNING KEEPSAKE

Three things I have learned in this lesson are:

1. _____

2. _____

3. _____

Something that helped me learn in this lesson was:

_____

_____

_____

As a result of this lesson, I will:

_____

_____

_____

LESSON 23

The Three Rs: Respect, Rights and Responsibilities

Learning outcome: 3.5

responsible resilient aware

By the end of this lesson you will:

→ realise that each person in a relationship has rights and responsibilities

→ have improved your assertive communication skills

KEYWORDS

Respect
Rights
Responsibilities

People in healthy relationships have rights and responsibilities. For example, you have a right to be treated with respect, but you also have the responsibility to treat the other person with respect too.

INDIVIDUAL ACTIVITY

Managing myself   Being social

1. Below are a list of rights that would be displayed and respected in a healthy relationship. Write down the responsibility that goes with each right.

YOU HAVE THE RIGHT TO ...	YOU HAVE THE RESPONSIBILITY TO ...
Be treated with respect – always	Treat someone with whom you are in a relationship with respect – always
Feel safe	
Enjoy friends and activities apart from the other person	
Express yourself honestly	
Express your culture and identity	
Express your opinions	
Say 'No'	
Be treated as an equal	
Feel comfortable being yourself	
Leave a relationship	
Privacy	

2. Now read the following entries from a diary by fifteen-year-old Jane. After you have read them, fill in the rights and responsibilities that Jane has in each situation.

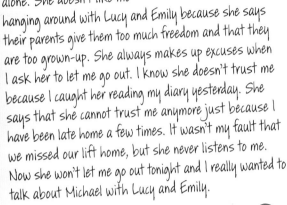

21 October

Dear Diary,

I don't know what to do. I was over in Michael's house last night watching a film, and his parents were out. We started kissing, and then Michael asked me to go upstairs in case his parents came back early. Before we could go upstairs, his parents came in and then Michael walked me home. I am supposed to be going over to his house again tonight and I don't know what I will do if he asks me to go upstairs. I don't really want to ...

31 October

Dear Diary,

I'm so upset. I think it's all off between me and Michael. Mr Higgs put me and Jim together to work on the science project. Mr Higgs thinks we might win a prize for the project and we've stayed back after school a couple of times to work on it. But Michael heard about it and is annoyed because Jim asked me ages ago to go out with him. He's asked me not to work on the project anymore, but when I said that the project was very important to me and to Jim, he stormed off and now he won't answer my calls or messages. Jim has messaged a couple of times wondering if the project is still on, but I just can't be bothered getting back to him right now.

1 November

Dear Diary,

My mother will not leave me alone. She doesn't like me hanging around with Lucy and Emily because she says their parents give them too much freedom and that they are too grown-up. She always makes up excuses when I ask her to let me go out. I know she doesn't trust me because I caught her reading my diary yesterday. She says that she cannot trust me anymore just because I have been late home a few times. It wasn't my fault that we missed our lift home, but she never listens to me. Now she won't let me go out tonight and I really wanted to talk about Michael with Lucy and Emily.

15 November

Dear Diary,

Lucy and Emily are always fighting and this time it's really serious. Lucy says that Emily is always copying everything she wears and that she cannot do anything for herself, and Emily's saying that Lucy is getting really big-headed and thinks she's great. I feel a bit bad because I told them what they said about each other, but it's really awkward because they both want me to take their side. To make things worse, we are all in the same Home Economics class and our teacher said we have to pick a partner for cookery for the year. Of course both of them have asked me to be their partner and now I feel sick just thinking about it.

DIARY ENTRY	JANE'S RIGHTS	JANE'S RESPONSIBILITIES
21 October		
31 October		
1 November		
15 November		

Listening and expressing myself

CLASS ACTIVITY

Answer the following questions and then discuss your answers as a class.

1. Do you think any of the people Jane wrote about intended to ignore her rights? Give reasons for your answer.

_____

_____

_____

2. Do you think Jane intended to ignore the rights of any of the people who featured in her diary entries? Give reasons for your answer.

_____

_____

_____

3. Choose an issue from one of Jane's diary entries – what advice would you give her?

_____

_____

_____

_____

RECAP: RIGHTS AND RESPONSIBILITIES

1. Everybody has rights.
2. Each right that a person has comes with a responsibility to others.
3. Each person has a right to express and assert their rights and a responsibility to respect the rights of others.
4. All relationships are about balancing rights and responsibilities.

Knowing myself   Writing for different purposes

INDIVIDUAL ACTIVITY

Choose one situation from your own life and write a diary entry describing how you expressed one of your own rights in a responsible manner. Name the right and the corresponding responsibility.

My Diary Entry

The situation: _____

_____

_____

_____

_____

_____

_____

_____

_____

My right: _____

My responsibility: _____

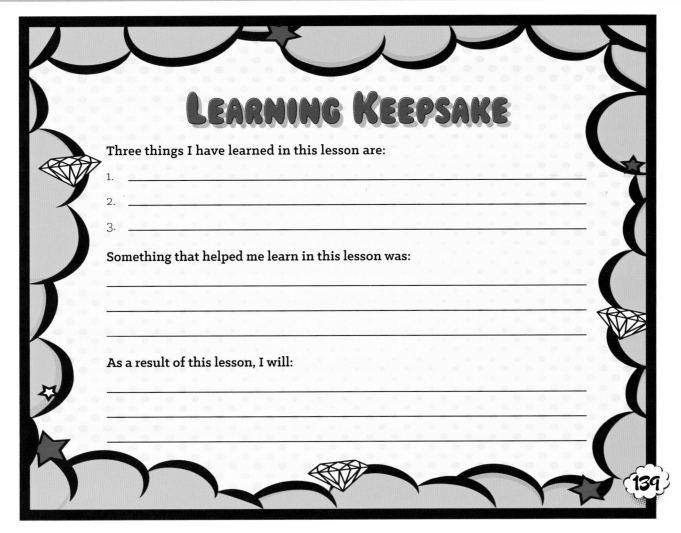

LEARNING KEEPSAKE

Three things I have learned in this lesson are:

1. _____

2. _____

3. _____

Something that helped me learn in this lesson was:

_____

_____

As a result of this lesson, I will:

_____

_____

LESSON 24 — Conflict and Breaking Up

Learning outcomes: 3.4, 3.5

responsible · resilient · connected · aware

By the end of this lesson you will:

↝ understand that breaking up is a natural part of growing up

↝ be able to identify the appropriate way to end a relationship

KEYWORDS

Breaking up

Communication

Conflict

USEFUL WEBSITE

www.kidshealth.org Provides advice on how to cope with a break-up and how to end a relationship respectfully.

Breaking up is hard to do

Being in a relationship can be a wonderful feeling. When you develop strong feelings for someone, you love being in their company and you can't wait to see them. It feels amazing that someone cares for you as much as you care for them. Some relationships can develop and last for months or years. However, sometimes relationships don't work out for any number of reasons and people will break up. When a relationship ends, it is hard for both people involved.

Learning
with others

Reading with
understanding

INDIVIDUAL ACTIVITY

Read this poem and then in groups discuss what you think it is about.

'The Thickness of Ice' by Liz Loxley

At first we'll meet as friends
(though secretly I'll be hoping
we'll become much more
and hoping that you're hoping that too).

At first we'll be like skaters
testing the thickness of ice
(with each meeting
we'll skate nearer the centre of the lake).

Later we'll become less anxious to impress,
less eager than the skater going for gold.
(The triple jumps and spins
will become an old routine:
we will become content with simple movements.)

Later we will not notice the steady thaw,
the creeping cracks will be ignored.
(And one day when the ice gives way
we will scramble to save ourselves
and not each other.)

After that we'll meet as acquaintances
(though secretly we'll be enemies
hurt by missing out on a medal,
jealous of new partners).

Last of all we'll be like children
having learnt the thinness of ice
(though secretly perhaps we may be hoping
to break the ice between us
and maybe meet again as friends).

Thinking creatively
and critically

Learning
with others

As a group, discuss and then add to the list of reasons why it is difficult to end a relationship and why it is difficult to accept that a relationship is ending or over.

IT IS DIFFICULT TO END A RELATIONSHIP BECAUSE . . .	IT IS DIFFICULT TO ACCEPT THAT A RELATIONSHIP IS ENDING BECAUSE . . .
You have mixed feelings about the person.	You feel hurt or rejected.

Why relationships end

Relationships break up for a number of reasons.

- You might grow apart; as you spend more time with someone, you may feel you are not as well matched as you thought you were.

- You might not be getting along and arguing a lot.

- You might develop feelings for someone else.

- You might not want to be tied to a serious relationship.

- You might not have the same feelings and for whatever reason you don't enjoy spending time with the other person anymore.

- You might have lost respect for the other person for whatever reason.

Knowing myself

INDIVIDUAL ACTIVITY

Read the following accounts from Sophie and Steven to hear two sides of a break-up story and then answer the questions that follow.

Sophie's side

Me and Steven have been going out together for the last seven months. I thought everything was going well. At the start he made every effort to meet me. He told me he preferred spending time with me to going out with his friends. I told him a lot of personal things, because I really trust him and I needed someone to talk to. Last month he started to meet me less and less. When I met him he made excuses about having a lot of rugby matches and he also said he had to mind his younger brother sometimes. But worst of all, yesterday at school he ignored me completely. My friends said they saw him with a girl from Fifth Year on Saturday night. I'm so upset. I want to say something to him but I am afraid he will break up with me if I do. I want to tell him I don't mind if I see him less as long as we can stay together.

Steven's side

I have been going out with Lucy for the last seven months. It was great at the start, but I just don't feel the same way now as I did then. Plus I fancy someone else. I tried to give Lucy some hints, but she is just not getting it. I feel really sorry for her after what she told me about her family and I don't want to break it off to her face. I'm just going to avoid her for a while and hopefully she will get the message. I really am busy with rugby at the moment so I can use that as an excuse.

1. What advice would you give to Lucy?

_____

_____

2. What advice would you give to Steven?

_____

_____

PAIR ACTIVITY

Now write a role-play in which Steven breaks up with Sophie in the right way. While one pair is doing the role-play, the rest of the class will fill in the observation sheet below.

Observation Sheet

1. How did Steven show that he still cares about Lucy's feelings even though they are breaking up?

   _____

   _____

2. How did Sophie show that she respects Steven's right to finish the relationship?

   _____

   _____

3. What could they both have done differently/better?

   _____

   _____

4. Based on the role-play, how will Sophie and Steven get on the next time they meet?

   _____

   _____

Dealing with heartbreak

Nearly everyone experiences a break-up at some point in their lives. Break-ups bring with them heartbreak. When you go through a break-up, you can feel a wide range of emotions: angry, hurt, rejected, confused, despairing and maybe even jealous. Break-up is a type of loss. You feel a sense of loss for the relationship, the friendship you had and the loss of what could have been. People may tell you to move on, that there are plenty more fish in the sea, but when it's happening to you it may feel that you will never get over it.

A break-up, although difficult, can also provide an opportunity to learn. It's not easy, but it's a chance to do your best to respect another person's feelings. It can be very hard, but it can help us to develop our skills when it comes to being honest and kind during difficult conversations.

Tips for getting over a break-up

☞ **Talk to someone.** Talking to someone you trust can help. It may make you feel better if someone can understand what you are going through.

☞ **Be good to yourself.** Even if you don't feel like it, try to eat all your meals, get some exercise and have a good sleep. If you find it difficult to sleep, try concentrating on your breath. This is a good way of getting off to sleep.

☞ **Distance yourself from the other person.** Don't text them or comment on their profile on social media. Don't follow their social media page, as it could upset you more if you see them moving on.

☞ **Try to keep positive.** When you break up with someone, your self-esteem can take a knock. Rejection is always difficult, no matter what age you are. Remember all the good qualities you have. Every night write down three good things about yourself.

☞ **Spend time with friends.** Spending time with friends can help distract you and cheer you up.

☞ **Keep yourself busy.** It can be difficult to motivate yourself when you are feeling down. You may feel like curling up under your duvet and hiding from the world, but this is not helpful. Try to do things to distract yourself or that usually made you happy.

☞ **Give yourself time.** It takes time to get over a break-up. When it happens, you may feel that you will never be happy again. Everyone has had their heart broken at some point and they have survived. Time is a healer and you will probably look back and wonder why you were so upset. You may, just may, even laugh about it all.

  # INDIVIDUAL ACTIVITY

Knowing myself Thinking creatively and critically

You have the right to end a relationship any time you want to, but you have a responsibility to do it in the right way. Write a list of Dos and Don'ts for ending a relationship.

DO	DON'T
Decide in advance what you want to say.	Get someone else to do it.
Put yourself in the other person's shoes.	'Ghost' the person – that is, ignore them completely and hope they get the hint.

Learning Keepsake

Three things I have learned in this lesson are:

1. _____

2. _____

3. _____

Something that helped me learn in this lesson was:

_____

_____

_____

As a result of this lesson, I will:

_____

_____

_____

MEET THE CHALLENGE
Strand 3 Topic 2
ADVICE BLOG ON RELATIONSHIPS

Learning outcome: 3.5

Working on your own, choose a relationship from TV, film or literature in which two young people are experiencing difficulty/conflict. Based on the relationship, write a blog post by an agony aunt/uncle giving advice on how these two young people can stay safe and responsible within their relationship. Follow these points in creating your blog post:

- ○ Plan your blog post before you start writing.

- ○ Give a headline that is both informative and will capture readers' attention.

- ○ Use images to enhance your post.

- ○ Edit your blog post. Make sure to avoid repetition. Read your post aloud to check it. Correct any punctuation or grammar mistakes.

- ○ Include where and how to get support if necessary.

TOPIC 3
Sexuality, Gender Identity and Sexual Health

Sexually Transmitted Infections

Learning outcome: 3.7

 responsible

 resilient

 connected

 aware

By the end of this lesson you will:

↝ know what an STI is

↝ know how to prevent an STI

↝ know how to seek treatment for an STI

KEYWORD

Sexually transmitted infection

USEFUL WEBSITES

www.sexualwellbeing.ie Provides advice and information about STIs.

www.b4udecide.ie Provides information about STIs.

www.hse.ie/eng/health/hl/yoursexualhealth/ Provides a wide range of information on sexual health and wellbeing.

What are STIs?

STIs are 'sexually transmitted infections'. They can be passed on:

- through sexual intercourse and/or close sexual contact with someone who is infected
- through sharing infected needles
- from a mother to her baby during pregnancy, childbirth or breastfeeding

The most common STIs in Ireland are chlamydia and genital warts.

Why is it important to learn about STIs?

- So that you are well informed and not misinformed.
- So that you make informed decisions about your behaviour.
- So that you look after your body and prevent possible health problems.
- So that you avoid serious long-term health consequences. Untreated STIs can result in infertility in both men and women.
- So that you can talk openly about STIs with a boyfriend or girlfriend.

Some common symptoms of STIs

- No symptoms
- Unusual discharge from penis, vagina or anus
- Pain when peeing
- Lumps or skin growths around the genital area
- Rash
- Unusual vaginal bleeding
- Itchy genitals or anus
- Blisters or sores around the genital areas or anus

These symptoms can also be caused by something other than an STI. A medical check-up and tests will diagnose the cause.

Some STIs have no noticeable symptoms and there may be no way of knowing whether or not a partner is infected. Despite the lack of visible symptoms, STIs can cause serious illness, infertility and even death, so it is extremely important to diagnose and treat STIs. If symptoms seem to disappear, the infection can still remain and the infected person can transmit the disease to others.

INDIVIDUAL ACTIVITY

Evaluating information

Read the statements about STIs and tick whether you think they are **true** or **false**. If you are **unsure**, tick the unsure box.

STATEMENT	TRUE	FALSE	UNSURE
You can prevent STIs by always wearing clean underwear and washing regularly.	☐	☐	☐
Once you have had an STI, you cannot get another one again.	☐	☐	☐
You can self-diagnose an STI.	☐	☐	☐
Anyone can get an STI.	☐	☐	☐
Condoms help prevent the spread of STIs.	☐	☐	☐
You can have more than one STI at the same time.	☐	☐	☐
You can catch an STI from toilet seats, water fountains or sharing cutlery.	☐	☐	☐
You can get an STI if you get a tattoo and the artist uses an infected needle.	☐	☐	☐
You cannot get an STI the first time you have sex.	☐	☐	☐
All STIs can be cured.	☐	☐	☐
If you know your partner well, you cannot get an STI.	☐	☐	☐
The symptoms of STIs are sometimes not noticeable.	☐	☐	☐
You can tell just by looking at someone whether or not they have an STI.	☐	☐	☐

Some common STIs

STIs can be viral, bacterial or parasitic. Viral STIs can be treated with medicines but not cured. Bacterial STIs can be cured with antibiotics. Parasitic STIs can be treated with creams and lotions. A lot of STIs have no noticeable symptoms so there may be no way of knowing if a partner is infected.

Chlamydia

- A bacterial infection
- May cause vaginal discharge/burning during urination
- Often no symptoms
- If not treated, it can lead to infertility
- Once treated it can be cured quickly and painlessly

Pelvic inflammatory disease

- Caused by an infection such as chlamydia spreading to other parts of the reproduction organs
- Can lead to infertility

Genital warts

- Caused by a virus called human papilloma virus
- Passed on by genital skin-to-skin contact
- Infects the skin
- Causes warts on the genital area
- No cure, but the warts can be removed
- Linked to cervical cancer

Genital herpes

- Caused by the virus that causes cold sores
- Can be passed on by skin-to-skin contact, kissing and sexual intercourse
- Unusual discharge, spots or red bumps around the genital area
- No treatment, but can be kept under control. Once contracted, the virus stays in the body and can become active again.

Gonorrhoea
('the clap')

- A bacterial infection
- Often has no symptoms in women, but can lead to infertility
- Unusual discharge
- Can be cured by antibiotics

Pubic lice
('crabs')

- Caused by parasites
- Cause itchiness in the infected area
- Can be passed on by skin-to-skin contact, shared bedding, towels and clothes
- Cured with lotions and shampoos similar to those used for head lice

Hepatitis B

- Caused by a virus that infects the liver
- Transmitted by contact with blood, semen, vaginal fluid or saliva
- A preventive vaccine is available

HIV
(human immunodeficiency virus)

- Virus that attacks the immune system
- May lead to AIDS
- No cure but can be managed with HIV medication

Syphilis

- A bacterial infection passed on through sexual contact
- Can have no symptoms, but where symptoms occur, can include painless sores or a rash
- No vaccine
- Treatable with antibiotics
- Treatment depends on how long the infection has been in the body

Scabies

- Caused by small insects called mites
- Passed on by skin-to-skin contact or sexual contact
- Can live for 72 hours outside the body so can be caught from clothing, bed sheets and towels
- Symptoms may not develop for six weeks
- Cause an intense itch
- Can be treated with creams and lotions

HIV – Know your facts

HIV (human immunodeficiency virus) is a virus that weakens the immune system. Our immune system helps us to fight off sickness and infections by attacking germs that enter the body. HIV cannot be cured but it can be treated effectively with medications. HIV treatment is a life-long treatment that prevents HIV reproducing in the body, and it enables most people with HIV to live long and otherwise healthy lives. AIDS (acquired immune deficiency syndrome) is caused by HIV. With the right treatment, a person with HIV will not develop AIDS.

PEP (post-exposure prophylaxis) is a course of medication that can be taken up to 72 hours after a person thinks they might have been exposed to the HIV virus. It reduces the chances of developing HIV.

Many people are unaware of the ways HIV can and cannot be transmitted. It is important to have the correct information and not believe rumours around how HIV is transmitted. Scaremongering (spreading frightening rumours) can lead to fear, stigma and discrimination for a person living with HIV.

You can get HIV by:

- having sex without a condom

- sharing needles

- being infected as a baby when in the womb, during childbirth or when breastfeeding, if the mother is not taking HIV treatment

- contaminated blood products

You cannot get HIV from:

- touching, hugging or kissing

- sharing cutlery or other utensils

- saliva, sweat or urine

- sharing a public toilet

Getting treatment for STIs

As mentioned above, despite the fact that some STIs have no visible symptoms, they can cause serious illness, infertility and even death if left untreated. It is extremely important to diagnose and treat STIs. Even if the symptoms seem to disappear, the infection can still remain and the infected person can transmit the infection to others. If a person thinks they may have an STI, it is important that they contact their doctor or local STI clinic. Once an STI has been diagnosed, partners also need to be treated, so that re-infection doesn't occur. Diagnosis and treatment for STIs can be simple and effective; however, there are no cures for some STIs so **prevention is very important**.

> Abstinence from sex and intimate sexual contact is the only way to give yourself 100% protection against sexually transmitted infections. Condoms can dramatically decrease the chances of someone getting an STI such as chlamydia, gonorrhoea or HIV; however, they do not offer complete protection from infections that are spread through skin-to-skin contact, such as herpes, syphilis and genital warts.

INDIVIDUAL ACTIVITY

Reflecting on and evaluating learning

Now test your knowledge by completing the following sentences.

FACTFILE

The most common STIs in Ireland are _____

The difference between viral and bacterial STIs is that _____
_____

The best way to avoid getting an STI altogether is _____

The best way to reduce the risk of getting an STI is _____

Common symptoms of STIs are _____
_____

The only way a person knows for sure if they have an STI is _____

If I thought I had an STI I would _____

If a friend told me they thought they had an STI I would _____

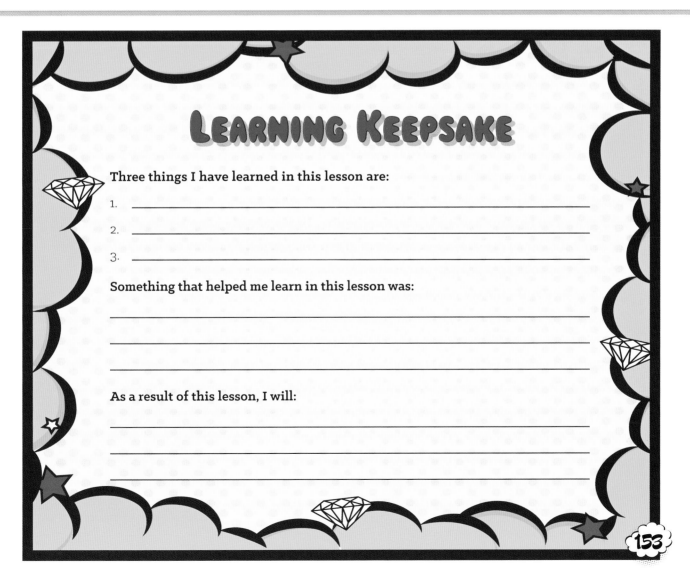

LEARNING KEEPSAKE

Three things I have learned in this lesson are:

1. _____

2. _____

3. _____

Something that helped me learn in this lesson was:

_____
_____
_____

As a result of this lesson, I will:

_____
_____
_____

LESSON 26 — Sexting

Learning outcomes: 3.7, 3.8

responsible · **connected** · **respected** · **aware**

By the end of this lesson you will:

- ✦ understand the consequences, both legal and emotional, of sexting
- ✦ demonstrate assertive communication and make informed decisions on how to deal with a sexting request
- ✦ examine whether males and females experience equal treatment online

KEYWORDS

Sexting

Sextortion

Revenge porn

USEFUL WEBSITES

www.hotline.ie Provides an anonymous facility for internet users to report suspected illegal content, particularly child sexual abuse material, in a secure and confidential way. The hotline is run in collaboration with An Garda Síochána and is overseen by the Department of Justice and Equality (the Office for Internet Safety).

www.childline.org.uk Provides information and advice on matters related to sexting.

Sexting

When people talk about sexting, they mean the sending, receiving or forwarding of sexually explicit messages, images, photographs or videos using mobile phones or digital devices. Teenagers probably know it best as trading naked picture or nudes. Sending a sexual text, image or video can be very dangerous, because once you send it, you have absolutely no control over what happens to it next.

The media often relays the message that sexting is 'out of control' among Irish teenagers. It is important, however, to realise that sexting is not something that everyone does.

INDIVIDUAL ACTIVITY

Being responsible, safe and ethical in digital technology

Read the statements about online communication and sexting and tick whether you **agree**, **disagree** or are **unsure.**

STATEMENT	AGREE	DISAGREE	UNSURE
It's no big deal to send nude pictures, it's harmless and just a bit of fun.	☐	☐	☐
Sexting is an important step if you want to take a relationship to the next level.	☐	☐	☐
The media are wrong; not that many teenagers are sexting.	☐	☐	☐
Sexting is against the law.	☐	☐	☐
If you are sent a nude picture, you don't need to worry, because it is on your phone and you can delete it.	☐	☐	☐
If something was shared with me online that upset me, I would know what to do.	☐	☐	☐
It's OK to send a nude photo on Snapchat, because it is temporary and disappears.	☐	☐	☐
Young people are under pressure to send nude pictures in relationships.	☐	☐	☐
It's OK to send a naked picture if the person's face isn't seen.	☐	☐	☐
Girls are more affected than boys by sexting.	☐	☐	☐
If you send a naked picture to someone and they don't share it, that is OK.	☐	☐	☐
If you really like a person and you know you can trust them, it is OK to send a sext.	☐	☐	☐
Forcing another person to send a sexual image or video or threatening them if they don't is extremely serious.	☐	☐	☐

Why do some young people sext?

There are a number of reasons why a person may decide to sext. They might:

- feel like joining in because they think everyone else is doing it, even if they are not

- feel under pressure from a boyfriend/girlfriend or friends

- feel it is easier to just 'give in' to someone who keeps asking

- find it difficult to say no if someone asks them for a nude

- be in love with or really like the person and trust them

- feel it is a form of flirting and are just testing out their sexual identity

- see it as a way to get attention

- feel it shows interest in a person they like or fancy

- be taking part in a game like 'Truth or Dare'

- feel they might be seen as 'frigid' or 'chicken' if they don't and go along with something, even though they are not comfortable with it

- feel proud of their body and want to show it off

- be worried that someone will lose interest or end a relationship if they don't send one

- feel harassed, threatened or blackmailed into sending a picture or more pictures (sextortion)

- feel threatened by an ex who already has sexual images of them (revenge porn)

> **Sextortion** is a form of blackmail. It is when a person threatens to post a sexual image or video online or share it with friends/family if they are not paid a sum of money or are not sent more sexual content.
>
> **Revenge porn** is sending sexually explicit images or video of individuals without their permission. The sexually explicit images or video may have been made with the exploited person's initial knowledge and consent, or they may have been made without his or her knowledge.
>
> Both sextortion and revenge porn are very serious crimes.

What does the law say?

- Sexting is illegal if you are under the age of 17. If you take, possess or distribute a sexual photograph of someone under 17, you have broken the law, even if the person in the photograph is the one who is taking, possessing or distributing the photo.

- In legal terms, a person under the age of 17 is considered a child.

- Any image that shows a child engaged in sexual activity or that focuses on the genital region of a child is sexually explicit and illegal (the Child Trafficking and Pornography Act 1998).

- Sharing someone's nude images or videos without their consent is against the law. Under the data protection law, individuals have the right not to have their personal data, including their image, collected or published without their consent.

A person under 17 is breaking the law if they

1. take a sexual picture or video of themselves or a friend (it is illegal to possess a sexual selfie)

2. share a sexual image or video of a person under 17, even if both parties are under 17

3. possess, download or store a sexual image or video of a person under 17 even if the person gave them permission to take it

INDIVIDUAL ACTIVITY

Reading with understanding

Read the following scenario featuring Sarah and complete the activities that follow it.

Sarah

Sarah is 14 and she has been seeing Tom for the last month. He is two years ahead of her in school. They were friends in First and Second Year but it was obvious to everyone that they really liked each other. Tom is a very popular boy in school and Sarah is very excited about going out with him. They spend most lunchtimes sitting together chatting and they hang out together at weekends. Most evenings Sarah spends her time after she has done her homework chatting with Tom. It's mostly fun and flirty. One evening while chatting back and forth with Tom, he sends the following text message.

Tom: So what are you up to

Sarah: I'm just getting ready for bed just out of the shower

Are you wearing anything

Ahhhh my towel

Id like to see whats under the towel send me a pic!!!

I don't think so

Go on its just between me and you.

I don't know

Go on I will send one

Sarah is very surprised by this text as Tom is not usually this forward or flirty. She is reluctant to send him a picture but she knows she really likes him and she trusts him. She has chatted to her friends before about this and they think sexting is normal and everyone is doing it.

CLASS DISCUSSION

Discussing/Debating

Do you think this is a realistic scenario?

What do you think Sarah is thinking/feeling?

Why do you think Tom asked for the picture?

Does Tom respect Sarah?

Sarah is reluctant to send the picture. Why might she end up sending it?

PAIR ACTIVITY

Thinking creatively and critically

In pairs, write down what could happen if Sarah sends the picture. Explore a wide range of consequences.

If Sarah sends the picture ...

INDIVIDUAL ACTIVITY

Reading with understanding

Now read Tom's side in this scenario and then participate in the class discussion.

Tom

Tom is 16 years old. He really likes Sarah and he enjoys the time they spend together. She is his first girlfriend. Tom sent a message to Sarah asking for a nude pic; he doesn't really know why, he was just a little bored and it seemed like a fun thing to do. Lately his friends have being joking with him about how hot Sarah is. Part of him thinks he could really impress the boys with this picture.

CLASS DISCUSSION

Discussing/Debating

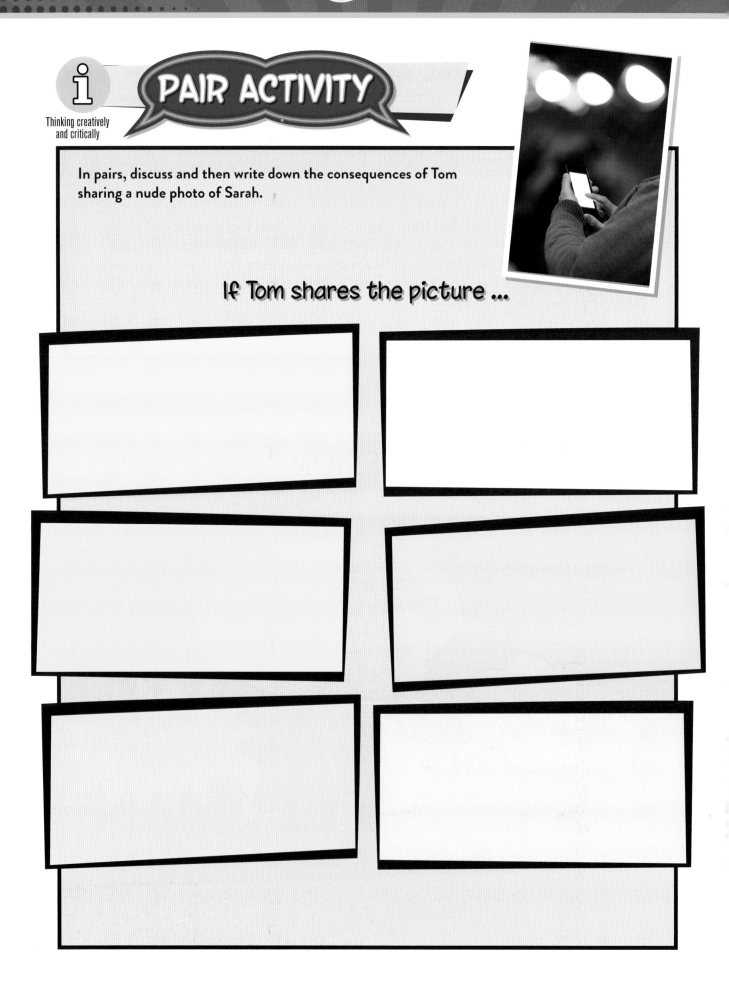

PAIR ACTIVITY

Thinking creatively and critically

In pairs, discuss and then write down the consequences of Tom sharing a nude photo of Sarah.

If Tom shares the picture ...

Being safe | **Exploring options and alternatives**

Now, in groups, decide how this scenario should end. Create a storyboard with a positive ending. Write the dialogue for Sarah and Tom underneath each box and then sketch in that scene in the story (you don't have to be able to draw well; you can use stick figures to represent Sarah and Tom).

1

_____

_____

_____

2

_____

_____

_____

3

_____

_____

_____

4

_____

_____

5

_____

_____

6

_____

_____

Advice for protecting yourself online

It's out of your control: Once you send a sext, you have no control over what happens to it. Once an image is out there, it can't be taken back. Deleting posts or messages is no safeguard against them having already been received, copied and sent to others.

Think about it: Any images that are stored or shared online can become public property. Think about how you would feel if your parents, classmates or neighbours saw the image. A good question to ask yourself is 'Would I be comfortable if my granny saw this picture?'

Don't be pressured: If you feel someone is putting you under pressure to send a naked picture, use some of the tips you have learned about resisting peer pressure.

- Be honest, use short clear statements: 'I don't want to, I'm not comfortable'.
- Expect the other person to accept your decision; if they care about you, they will.
- Block the sender if the pressure is persistent and you feel threatened by it.

Don't trust everyone: We can never be 100% sure that the person we send the photograph to will not pass it on. People who swear to never share a photo can and do break their promise, whether deliberately or accidentally. In some cases a person you only met online may not be who they say they are, and images can get into the wrong hands.

Remember it's illegal: If you are under 17, both sending and receiving sexts is **illegal**. It is also illegal to possess a sexual selfie.

Talk to a trusted adult: Report any explicit or sexual pictures you receive to a parent or a trusted adult; they can help you do the right thing. The same goes if you have sent a sexual image and you are worried about it. **Facing up to a problem is never as bad as you think it will be.**

Don't resend: If you receive an explicit text, don't share it with anyone. To do so is 'non-consensual' sharing and is **against the law**. Sending on a picture can cause a lot of harm to the person in the image. It is a betrayal of someone's trust and can seriously affect them emotionally. Think about how the other person might feel if someone else saw it. Think about how you would feel if it was a picture of you.

IF YOU FEEL THREATENED

If you feel you are a victim of sextortion or of revenge porn (and remember, these are both crimes):

1. Don't share more images or pay money.

2. Look for help, talk to a trusted adult.

3. Keep the evidence, don't delete anything, save messages, take screenshots.

4. Block the person. Don't delete your account.

5. Report it to An Garda Síochána.

▶ YouTube

Go to YouTube and look up 'Exposed Education film for CEOP' (10:34). This is an informative piece on sexting that shows you that facing up to things is never as bad as you think it is.

INDIVIDUAL ACTIVITY

Being responsible, safe and ethical in using digital technology

Imagine your friend has texted you to say they are thinking of sending a nude picture to someone. From what you learned in this lesson, send back a text to convince them that this is a bad idea.

They've asked me to send a naked selfie – I think I will!

LEARNING KEEPSAKE

Three things I have learned in this lesson are:

1. _____

2. _____

3. _____

Something that helped me learn in this lesson was:

_____

_____

_____

As a result of this lesson, I will:

_____

_____

_____

LESSON 27

Consent

Learning outcome: 3.8

responsible , resilient , respected , aware

By the end of this lesson you will:

• understand what consent and intimacy mean
• understand the importance of communication, especially in establishing consent in relationships

KEYWORD

Consent

USEFUL WEBSITE

www.b4udecide.ie Provides information on consent and the law.

Being in a romantic relationship is a great feeling, but relationships can be difficult to navigate when intimacy, sex or sexual activity, which can involve kissing, sexual touching and sexual intercourse, come into the picture. Getting to know somebody and being open about your comfort levels around intimacy are essential to having a healthy, respectful relationship. Therefore, the matter of consent – seeking or giving permission and agreeing to something happening – is hugely important.

GROUP ACTIVITY

Listening and expressing myself

As a group, write down different situations where consent is needed in everyday life.

Consent in everyday life

Intimacy

Different people have different comfort levels around intimacy in relationships. What one person is comfortable or ready for, another may not be. This is why it is essential to talk to each other about what each person is comfortable doing. These types of conversation are an important part of consent for sexual activity.

Knowing myself   Being safe

INDIVIDUAL ACTIVITY

Read the statements about consent and tick whether you think each one is **true** or **false**.

STATEMENT	TRUE	FALSE
In Ireland, the age of consent (i.e. the age at which it is legal to have sex) is 17.	☐	☐
Consent is important in any type of sexual activity, e.g. kissing, touching or sexual intercourse.	☐	☐
Consent cannot be given if a person feels pressured, forced or threatened.	☐	☐
Once a person consents to a sexual activity, they cannot change their mind.	☐	☐
If a person agrees to a sexual act, they have to agree to it every time.	☐	☐
When kissing or touching your boyfriend/ girlfriend, it is important to check in with each other and know what both of you are comfortable and OK with.	☐	☐
Once a person is asleep, they cannot consent to a sexual activity.	☐	☐
If a couple aged 16 have sex, they are breaking the law.	☐	☐
A person can change their mind before or during any sexual activity.	☐	☐
If a person pushes you away, they are not giving consent.	☐	☐
Forcing someone to engage in something they do not want to is sexual assault.	☐	☐
A person cannot consent to sexual activity if they are impaired by the effects of drugs or alcohol.	☐	☐

What is sexual consent?

- Consent means agreeing to participate in an activity and understanding what is being agreed to.

- Consent must be freely given and never assumed.

- Consent should be part of an ongoing conversation, as what a person may consent to at one time, they may not consent to at a later date. Also, people will have different comfort levels around intimacy in relationships at different times in the relationship.

The Criminal Law (Sexual Offences) Act 2017 states that 'a person consents to a sexual act if he or she freely and voluntarily agrees to engage in that act'. The Act provides several circumstances under which consent cannot be given, including being asleep or unconscious; under force or the threat of force; or being impaired by alcohol or drugs. The law also clarifies that the list is not exhaustive.

The legal age of consent in Ireland

The law states that you must be 17 to consent to (agree to) have sexual intercourse. The age of consent is the same for males and females and is the same for homosexual and heterosexual sex.

What does this law mean?

This means that under the age of 17, you are not legally old enough to consent to sexual intercourse. In certain circumstances, someone who has sex under the age of 17 or with someone under the age of 17 may be prosecuted by the Gardaí.

Why does this law exist?

This law exists to protect people under the age of 17, who are more vulnerable than those aged 17 and over. People under the age of 17 are not considered by the law to be able to make the decision to consent to sex. The law aims to protect young people with these guidelines. It also aims to prevent older, more experienced people taking advantage and influencing the decisions of those younger than them.

Does this mean that a couple will go to jail if they have sex under 17?

This question cannot be answered for certain. It depends on a number of factors. A girl under 17 cannot be prosecuted under the legislation. But strictly speaking, a boy can be prosecuted for having sex under 17. The Gardaí and the Director of Public Prosecutions use their discretion and tend to look at the overall circumstances of a relationship before deciding whether or not to prosecute. The welfare of the young person is always the most important issue.

(Source: www.B4uDecide.ie/the-facts/age-of-consent/)

INDIVIDUAL ACTIVITY

Reading with understanding

Read the following story and participate in the class discussion that follows it.

A STORY OF CONSENT?

Jamie (18) and Alex (17) have been in a relationship for four months. The relationship has been going very well, but lately Alex has noticed changes in Jamie's behaviour. On a few occasions, while flirting on the phone, Jamie has asked Alex for a sexy selfie. Alex has felt uncomfortable about this and has tried to laugh off these requests in the hope that Jamie will get the hint, but Alex is not sure that Jamie has, because the requests keep coming.

One night, Jamie invites Alex to watch a movie, while Jamie's parents are out. They end up kissing on the couch, and Jamie starts to unbutton Alex's trousers. Alex really likes Jamie but isn't ready to move that fast. Not wanting to hurt Jamie's feelings, Alex pushes Jamie's hand away, but keeps kissing, hoping that Jamie will get the message to stop. Jamie expects Alex to just say 'no' or 'stop' if something isn't OK. So Jamie continues.

CLASS DISCUSSION

Discussing/Debating

REMEMBER:

- In Ireland the legal age of consent is 17.
- Consent means to give permission or to agree for something to happen.
- Consent should be mutual, voluntary and freely given.
- Consent should be continual. Just because a person has engaged in a specific activity in the past, it does not mean that they want to engage it in again – giving consent once is not a lifetime agreement.
- The only way of knowing that someone is consenting is if they tell you. It should not be presumed.
- It is the responsibility of both partners to check in by asking 'Is this OK with you?', 'Would you like it if ... ?', etc. Examples of body language which shows a person is not comfortable with what is going on include, but are not limited to: not responding to the other person's touch; pushing the other person away; holding their arms around themselves; stiffening up; turning away.
- In a situation where you feel the other person isn't listening to you or you feel unsafe, try to remove yourself from the situation.

LEARNING KEEPSAKE

Three things I have learned in this lesson are:

1. _____

2. _____

3. _____

Something that helped me learn in this lesson was:

_____

_____

_____

As a result of this lesson, I will:

_____

_____

_____

MEET THE CHALLENGE
Strand 3 Topic 3
RAISING AWARENESS ABOUT THE DANGERS OF SEXTING

Learning outcomes: 3.4, 3.8

You have been given the task of raising awareness about the dangers of sharing explicit images online. You can choose to do any of the following.

1. Design and make a poster

2. Create an information leaflet or magazine article

3. Create a video

4. Create a PowerPoint presentation

○ Include the following in the information you provide:

   ○ What is sexting?

   ○ What are the consequences of sexting, both legally and personally?

   ○ The consequences of 'non-consensual' sharing

   ○ Tips on how to make informed decisions to resist pressure to sext

   ○ Help and advice for someone who has already sent a sext.

○ Ensure that the different sections are clearly identifiable.

○ Ensure your presentation is attractive and easy to understand for the target audience.

○ Ensure that the information is clear and enhanced by design elements such as images and colour.

○ Ensure that the design is respectful of the topic.

LESSON 28
Media Influences on Relationships and Sexuality

Learning outcomes: 3.10, 3.11

 responsible

 connected

 aware

 respected

By the end of this lesson you will:

•► be more aware of the different types of media that impact on and influence your life

•► assess the use and overuse of sexual imagery in the media

•► identify gender stereotyping in the media and its impact on our perception of what it is to be male or female

•► recognise and critically examine the many ways in which the media influence your understanding of sexuality and sexual health

 **KEYWORDS**

Sexuality

Media influence

Sexual objectification

The media

'Media' refers to the various channels through which we receive information. We encounter media in many different forms, such as print media (books, magazines, newspapers), television, radio, movies, video games, music, billboards, the internet, mobile phones and social media websites.

We depend on the media for information on everything – what's happening in the world, what new technology has been developed, what the latest fashion trends are, the latest music, the best places to eat, the most exciting places to go … the list is endless.

INDIVIDUAL ACTIVITY

Thinking creatively
and critically

Examining one day in your life, fill in the various forms of media that you encounter throughout that day in the table below, and at what times during the day. Also, fill in your reasons why you have accessed this form of media; for example, in the morning while eating breakfast, you might listen to a radio station or watch morning TV for entertainment/news/music; waiting at the bus stop, you might read a billboard advert to pass the time.

TIME OF DAY	TYPE OF MEDIA	REASON WHY

CLASS DISCUSSION

Discussing/Debating

Media influence

Whether we realise it or not, the effect of the media on us is far-reaching. It plays a part in shaping our behaviour. While we can benefit from what the media has to offer, we need to be aware of its influence and the messages and values that are being presented to us. Only by being aware can we manage the influence it has on us.

Positive influence

The media can be a positive influence for teenagers.

- Teenagers who take an interest in the news are more likely to be interested in major social and political issues. This can be an educational experience and encourage teenagers to be more socially conscious and involved in their communities.

- Teenagers can find important information and advice about their health and wellbeing in the media; for example, messages aimed at preventing youth depression, encouraging healthy eating and lifestyle habits, and promoting positive, respectful relationships. Remember, however, that to keep the influence of media positive, it is important to safely access reliable websites or information sources.

Negative influence

Direct and indirect influence

Media influence on behaviour can be **direct**. Advertisers – who use many forms of media to sell us their products – use persuasive techniques that encourage us to buy the latest brands, gadgets or labels. They try to convince us that we need the products and that our lives will be better if we have them.

Influences can also be **indirect** – we are sometimes not aware of these messages. Through imagery and other tactics, advertisers give us subtle, hidden messages about the value/attractiveness/desirability of their products, and, more important, how we too might be valuable/attractive/desirable if we purchase their products.

Sexual objectification

Exposure to sexual imagery and content in the media can shape our attitudes, behaviour and values about gender roles and sexuality. Whether it is in movies, TV shows, music videos, lyrics or video games, we are constantly bombarded with content that is of a sexual nature.

Often males and females are **sexually objectified** in the media. Sexual objectification is where a person is seen only as an object of sexual desire; little regard is given to their personality or dignity. We have all seen advertisement of the partly dressed woman advertising perfume or the sculpted man selling aftershave. More focus is given to the model than to the product itself.

We have become so used to sexual imagery and content in the media that they no longer shock us and we accept them as normal. We need to realise that this imagery and content is far from normal and is especially detrimental to adolescents, who are still in a significant development stage of life where they are learning and developing their gender roles, sexual attitudes and sexual behaviours.

GROUP ACTIVITY

Thinking creatively and critically

When sexuality is used in advertising, certain values and attitudes towards sex and sexuality are being sold along with the product. As a group, examine the messages that these advertisers give us about sex and sexuality and then as a class participate in a discussion around them.

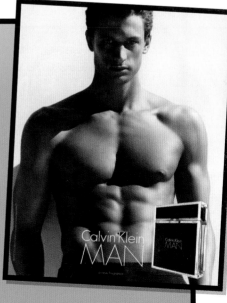

CLASS DISCUSSION

Discussing/Debating

GROUP ACTIVITY

Thinking creatively
and critically

Certain attitudes or opinions about gender and how men and women are and should act are also often used in advertising. In your group, examine the messages the advertisers give us about gender roles and then answer the questions that follow.

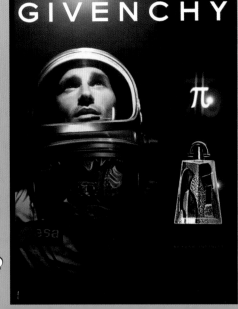

1. According to the advert, what type of man will you be if you use Givenchy Pi aftershave?

2. What underlying message does this give us about men and their worth?

3. According to the advert, what type of woman will you be if you wear these jeans?

4. What underlying message does this give us about women and their worth?

5. Do you think that these advertisements represent men and women in a fair and accurate way? Why/why not?

PAIR ACTIVITY

Thinking creatively and critically

In pairs, examine this advertisement and then answer the questions that follow.

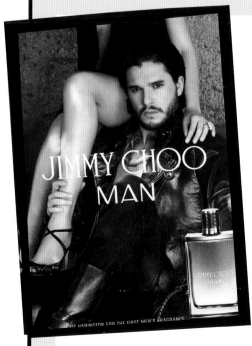

1. What do you think the advertiser is trying to achieve by using this image for the advert?

2. What does this message convey about women?

3. What does the message convey about men?

_____

_____

4. What messages does the advert give about sex and sexuality?

_____

_____

5. How do you feel about the advert?

_____

_____

6. Do you think this advertisement could influence how men and women view each other?

_____

_____

7. Have you seen an advert like this in real life? If so, what was it advertising?

_____

_____

 CLASS DISCUSSION

Discussing/Debating

Thinking creatively
and critically

GROUP ACTIVITY

As a group, select one form of media from the wheel and decide on a specific product of that form of media (i.e. pick a specific song/video/TV show, etc.). Then discuss the questions given about that product in the larger wheel below and write in your answers in the relevant segments.

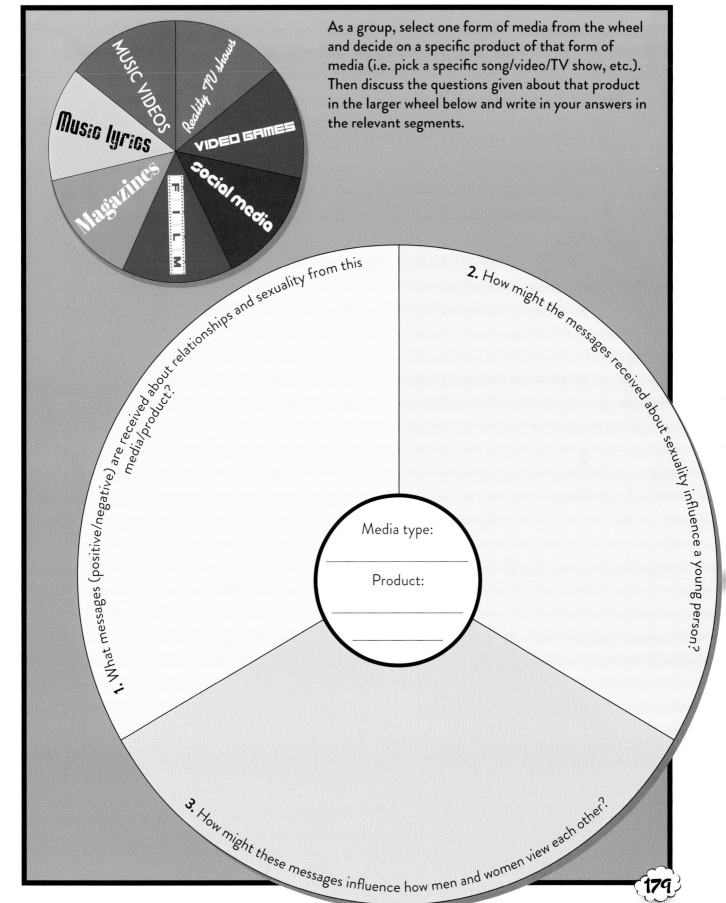

MUSIC VIDEOS

Reality TV shows

Music lyrics

VIDEO GAMES

Magazines

F I L M

social media

1. What messages (positive/negative) are received about relationships and sexuality from this media/product?

2. How might the messages received about sexuality influence a young person?

3. How might these messages influence how men and women view each other?

Media type:

Product:

LEARNING KEEPSAKE

Three things I have learned in this lesson are:

1. _____

2. _____

3. _____

Something that helped me learn in this lesson was:

_____

_____

_____

As a result of this lesson, I will:

_____

_____

_____

MY MENTAL HEALTH

STRAND 4

TOPIC 1
Dealing with Tough Times

Positive and Negative Stress

Learning outcome: 4.2

 responsible
 connected
 resilient
 aware

By the end of this lesson you will:

•→ have analysed what causes you stress in your life

•→ appreciate the role of stress in your life

•→ understand how different levels of stress can affect performance

KEYWORDS

Stress

Stressor

USEFUL WEBSITES

www.kidshealth.org Provides information on managing and reducing stress.

www.yourmentalhealth.ie Offers tips through the 'Little Things' campaign on reducing stress and improving wellbeing.

What is stress?

Stress is your body's physical and emotional reaction to pressure or threat. Stress can be necessary in life, and a certain amount of stress is essential in order to perform well, complete tasks and achieve our goals. However, too much stress is not a good thing. If we deal with stress early, it prevents it from becoming an overwhelming problem.

Knowing
myself

INDIVIDUAL ACTIVITY

Write down the things, events or situations that cause you stress. When your teacher takes feedback from the class, add in some situations that cause other people in your class stress. Circle anything that other people have come up with that you don't find particularly stressful.

WHAT CAUSES ME STRESS

WHAT CAUSES MY CLASSMATES STRESS

As you can see from this activity, stress means different things to different people, and our response to stress can vary too. What might be stressful for one person may not be for another. For example, a person might find performing on stage stressful and another person might savour the experience. We all respond differently depending on the situation we are in.

It is important to be able to manage our stress; the first step is recognising how much stress we are under.

Levels of stress and performance

As you have already learned, stress can be a positive thing in our lives. Our ability to perform increases up to a certain level of stress. There is a point at which we are under just enough pressure to perform to the maximum of our ability. Anything more than that level can make us stressed out. When this happens, we experience 'stress overload'. The diagram below shows the effects of stress on performance.

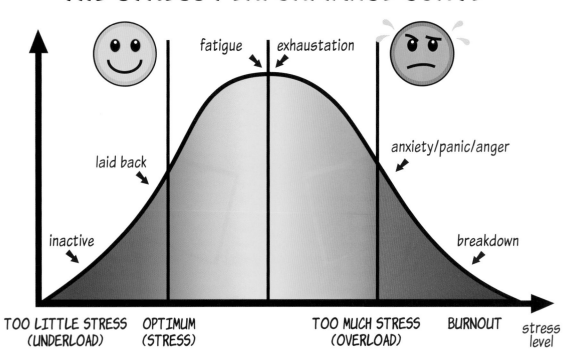

THE STRESS PERFORMANCE CURVE

fatigue   exhaustation

laid back

inactive

anxiety/panic/anger

breakdown

TOO LITTLE STRESS (UNDERLOAD)   OPTIMUM (STRESS)   TOO MUCH STRESS (OVERLOAD)   BURNOUT   stress level

TOO LITTLE STRESS	ENOUGH STRESS	TOO MUCH STRESS
● Too little pressure ● Too little challenge ● You are bored or lacking in motivation ● You are too laid-back ● You find it difficult to rise to challenges and reach your goals ● You do not have enough pressure to get things done, so other things take priority ● You are under-stimulated ● You do not perform at your best	● A healthy level of stress ● You are alert, energetic and enthusiastic ● You are motivated to achieve your goals ● At this level of stress you perform at your best ● A target or a deadline spurs you on	● You feel unable to cope with the pressure ● You feel overwhelmed, anxious, demotivated ● You have difficulty concentrating ● You can't meet daily challenges ● You do not perform at your best

INDIVIDUAL ACTIVITY

Knowing myself

Imagine these two scenarios and write into the graphs what you think might happen if the person was experiencing too little stress, just enough stress and too much stress.

SCENARIO 1:
MAKING A PRESENTATION

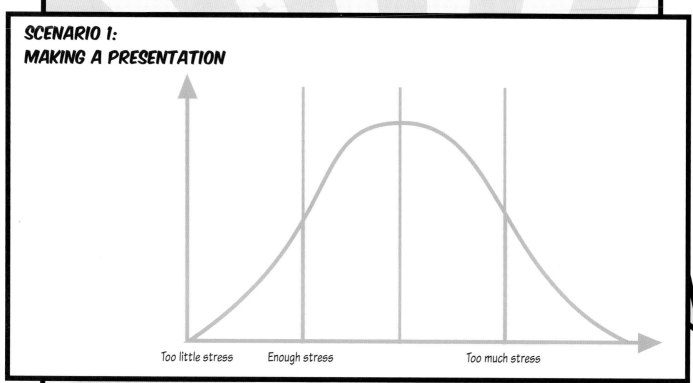

SCENARIO 2:
PREPARING FOR AN EXAM

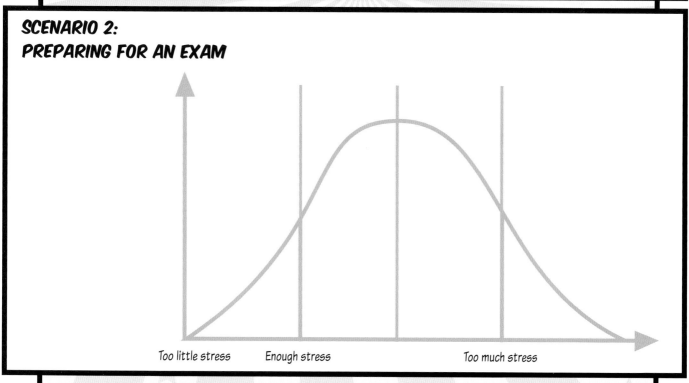

Learning Keepsake

Three things I have learned in this lesson are:

1. _____

2. _____

3. _____

Something that helped me learn in this lesson was:

_____

_____

_____

As a result of this lesson, I will:

_____

_____

_____

LESSON 30

Managing Stress in Our Lives

Learning outcomes: 4.2, 4.3, 4.8, 4.9

responsible · resilient · connected · aware

By the end of this lesson you will:

- have identified the signs of stress
- know the symptoms of too much stress
- have further developed the skills to help you manage challenges in your life

KEYWORDS

Symptoms

Behaviour

Physical effects

USEFUL WEBSITES

www.kidshealth.org Provides information on managing and reducing stress.

www.yourmentalhealth.ie Offers tips through the 'Little Things' campaign on reducing stress and improving wellbeing.

In the previous lesson, you learned about what causes us stress and the effects of stress on our performance in different situations. You cannot avoid all stress in your life, but you can learn to manage your stress levels. In order to successfully manage stress, it is important to be able to identify what is causing you stress. It is also essential to listen to what your body is telling you and how it is feeling.

Knowing myself

Being healthy

INDIVIDUAL ACTIVITY

When you feel under a lot of stress and pressure, your body reacts physically. Beside the picture below, write down how you think a person's body might react physically to stress and then share your answers as a class.

Dizziness

Face feels hot, flushed

CLASS DISCUSSION

Discussing/Debating

Feeling stressed: The stress response

Thousands of years ago, stress was essential for survival. Our ancestors were often in danger of attack from wild animals such as wolves and bears. The **stress response** allowed them to respond to the threat of attack by preparing them for 'fight or flight'.

Today, this fight-or-flight response works well in situations like running away from a vicious dog. However, most of the threats in today's world are much less obvious and sometimes our stress response kicks in during exams, conflicts with parents and in relationships with friends. In these situations, neither fight nor flight is an appropriate response, but our body still acts in the same supercharged way.

NORMAL RESPONSES TO STRESSFUL SITUATIONS

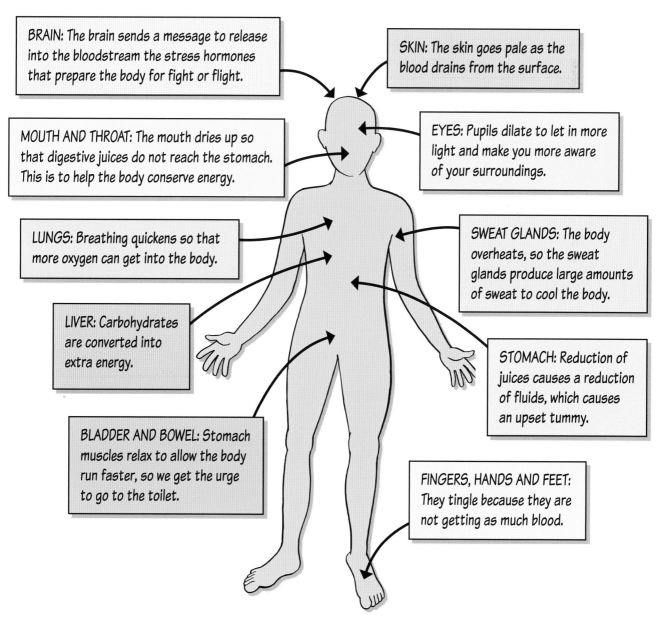

BRAIN: The brain sends a message to release into the bloodstream the stress hormones that prepare the body for fight or flight.

SKIN: The skin goes pale as the blood drains from the surface.

MOUTH AND THROAT: The mouth dries up so that digestive juices do not reach the stomach. This is to help the body conserve energy.

EYES: Pupils dilate to let in more light and make you more aware of your surroundings.

LUNGS: Breathing quickens so that more oxygen can get into the body.

SWEAT GLANDS: The body overheats, so the sweat glands produce large amounts of sweat to cool the body.

LIVER: Carbohydrates are converted into extra energy.

STOMACH: Reduction of juices causes a reduction of fluids, which causes an upset tummy.

BLADDER AND BOWEL: Stomach muscles relax to allow the body run faster, so we get the urge to go to the toilet.

FINGERS, HANDS AND FEET: They tingle because they are not getting as much blood.

Stress does not just affect us physically; it also affects our thoughts, feelings and behaviours. It is important to recognise the symptoms of stress early as the effects of stress can be harmful if they go on for too long. If we do not deal with our stress, it can be harmful to our physical and mental health.

Knowing myself

Being healthy

INDIVIDUAL ACTIVITY

Here are some common signs and symptoms of too much stress in our lives. Tick those you often experience and put an X beside those you rarely experience. Add in any other symptoms you can think of.

FEELINGS	✔/✗	THOUGHTS	✔/✗	BEHAVIOUR	✔/✗
Irritability		'I can't see an end to this'		Crying excessively	
Hopelessness		'I can't do this'		Nail-biting	
Anger		'My problems are huge'		Avoiding contact with other people	
Overwhelmed		'I'm useless'		Using illegal drugs or drinking	
Low mood		'I'm bored'		Overeating	
Edginess or feeling wound up		'I'm fed up'		Losing temper	
Short-tempered		'I can't do anything right'		Becoming accident-prone	

Thinking positively about stress

We cannot eliminate or avoid all stressful situations in our lives, but we can learn to control our reaction to stress. How we think and behave in certain situations can determine how stressful the situation will become. When we are stressed, it is very important to stay in control and think positively.

INSTEAD OF THINKING NEGATIVELY ...   **... THINK POSITIVELY**

I've got so much to do; I'll never get it done.

I have a lot to do, but if I take one thing at a time I will get it done.

Stress management techniques

Now that you can recognise the signs of stress, it is important to listen to your body and realise when you are becoming too stressed. There are a variety of stress management techniques to get you through stressful times. It is important to find things that work best for you.

avoid

We cannot avoid all stressful situations in our lives, but if the stress is causing you problems, sometimes it can be better for you to walk away from the situation. Learn to say no to things that you know will cause you stress. Try to avoid people who stress you out. For example, if one of your friends keeps trying to encourage you to drink, avoid the situation where that might occur.

alter

If you cannot avoid the stressor (the thing causing you the stress), try to change something in your life that will help you deal with the stress. If exams cause you a lot of stress, try to figure out what you can do to prevent this happening. Maybe you might need to manage your time better in the lead-up to exams. If someone is causing you stress, don't bottle it up; tell them honestly how you are feeling. Being honest about how you feel sometimes can really alleviate stress.

How to manage stress using the 4 As

adapt

If you cannot change what is causing you stress, you may need to change the way you think about it. Try to view stressful situations from a more positive perspective. Take things one step at a time. Tell yourself that this stress will pass and you will get through it. Put the stressor into perspective. Ask yourself, will this matter in a year, or even in a month? Reflect on things that have caused you stress in the past, and how that stress passed.

accept

Many things in life are beyond our control and some stressors are unavoidable. You can't change them or prevent them from happening. For example, parents separating, family bereavements and family illness are all major factors of stress that you cannot avoid, adapt or alter. It is important in these situations to learn to manage your stress and not let it control you. Sharing how you are feeling with a trusted adult or friend can be very beneficial even if there is nothing you can do to change the situation.

Looking after ourselves

Managing stress is not all about dealing with stress when it arises. There are other things we can do in our daily lives that can help prevent stress from causing problems. Taking care of ourselves is one of the most important things we can do to manage stress. This in turn can help us cope better with stress in our lives if it happens.

Eat healthily: If our bodies are nourished we are better able to cope with stress. Pay attention to what you are eating. Eat balanced, nutritious meals during the day. Cut down on junk food.

Take regular exercise: Taking regular exercise plays a key role in reducing and preventing the effects of stress. Take part in physical activity for 60 minutes each day.

Manage time effectively: Poor time management can cause a lot of stress. Make sure you don't take on too much or put things off until the last minute.

Get enough rest and sleep: Getting a good night's sleep fuels your mind as well as your body. If you are alert you are better able to cope with challenges. Feeling tired may increase your stress levels.

Avoid alcohol, cigarettes and drugs: These may seem like an option to escape stress but they cause bigger problems in the long run.

Spend time with people you like: Spending time with positive people can help you to have a positive outlook.

Reduce intake of caffeine and sugar: Caffeine and sugar give you a temporary high, which is followed by a crash in mood and energy. Reducing coffee, tea, soft drinks, chocolate and sweet snacks in our diet can help us to feel more relaxed and to sleep better.

Keep your sense of humour: The act of laughing can really help to manage stress.

Set aside time for things you enjoy: Making time for leisure activities that you enjoy can help you de-stress, relax and recharge your batteries. It could be walking the dog, reading, doing a crossword, listening to music – whatever it is that you enjoy doing.

Knowing myself

Being healthy

INDIVIDUAL ACTIVITY

Consider how you deal with stress in your life by completing the following questions.

The things that cause me stress in my life are:

_____

_____

_____

When I am stressed I feel:

_____

_____

_____

I can avoid stress by:

_____

_____

_____

_____

Three ways I could cope better with stress are:

1. _____

2. _____

3. _____

Stress Management Bingo

Play 'Stress Management Bingo'! Try some of these stress management tips, crossing them off as you complete them. They can help you de-stress and feel good about yourself.

Ask for help with a problem.

Spend time doing your favourite hobby.

Choose a healthy snack over junk food.

Get 8–9 hours' sleep each night.

Talk to someone about something that's bothering you.

Catch up with a friend.

Look up jokes that make you laugh.

Start reading a new book.

Practise a deep breathing exercise.

Exercise every day for one hour.

Say something positive to yourself on waking up each morning.

Learn to do something new.

Write down three things that you are happy for every night.

Make a to-do list each day.

Do homework straight away after school.

Spend time in nature.

Listen to music.

Watch a good film with your family.

Laugh out loud.

Clean out your wardrobe.

Do something that makes you happy.

Organise your notes.

Take a photo of something that makes you feel good.

Drink enough water every day.

Complete a crossword or puzzle.

Learning Keepsake

Three things I have learned in this lesson are:

1. _____

2. _____

3. _____

Something that helped me learn in this lesson was:

_____

_____

_____

As a result of this lesson, I will:

_____

_____

_____

LESSON 31

Relaxation

Learning outcomes: 2.1, 4.3

responsible · aware · resilient

By the end of this lesson you will:
- appreciate the importance of relaxation
- have learned and practised some relaxation techniques

KEYWORDS

The Relaxation Response

Guided relaxation

In order to be healthy it is important to balance physical and mental activity with rest and relaxation. If we are very busy, we can experience stress. It is important to have some stress-releasing activities to help us stay calm during stressful times.

To the right is a variety of different activities which you could use to relax. Circle the ones which you already use. Add in any that you do that are not mentioned.

50 Ways to Relax

Take a nap · Walk outside · Read a book · Take a bike ride · Take deep belly breaths · Learn something new · Play cards · Do Sudoku · Rest your legs up on a wall · Listen to a guided relaxation · Make some music · Take a bath · Meditate · View some art · Turn off all electronics · Take a walk · Take a tea/coffee break · Write a quick poem · Go to a park · Write a letter · Write in a journal · Call a friend · Watch the clouds · Play with a pet · Complete a crossword · Engage in small acts of kindness · Go for a run · Colour with crayons · Light a candle · Listen to music · Laugh out loud · Take a shower · Fly a kite · Find a relaxing scent · Read or watch something funny · Watch the stars · Read some poetry · Let go of something · Squeeze a stress ball · Put on some music and dance · Do some gentle stretches · Eat a meal in silence · Go for a swim · Give thanks · Let out a yell · Do some mindfulness colouring · Drink herbal tea · Forgive someone · Let out a sigh · Sit in nature

Learning to relax: The relaxation response

In the previous lesson, we learned about the stress response. The relaxation response is the opposite of the stress response – it is our ability to manage when we start to feel stressed, so that we can move to a state of calmness. When it is activated:

● our heart rate slows down

● our breathing becomes slower and more controlled

● our muscles become relaxed

● blood flow to the brain increases

You are now going to try some relaxation techniques which can activate the relaxation response. There is no single technique that suits everyone. It's only by trying them out that you can decide which ones are best for you. Practising these relaxation techniques for 10–20 minutes every day can help you to reduce and manage stress in your life. Be aware that your attention will wander and you may feel that it is too much hassle to do them every day, but with practice and dedication will come the benefits, both physical and mental, of activating our relaxation response.

1. Deep breathing exercise

When people become overwhelmed they can often forget to breathe. Deep breathing can really help a person cope with a stressful situation.

Get comfortable, sitting upright on a chair or lying on the floor on a mat …Place your hand on your abdomen … Take a slow deep breath in through your nose, noticing your hand moving outwards … Hold your breath for a count of three, then breathe out … Concentrate on your breathing. Notice that as you breathe out the tension is released … The calmest or quietest time in this process is immediately after you breathe out … Take note of the calmness in your body at this point … Repeat this three times.

2. Breathing exercise

Another simpler breathing exercise that you can use if you're feeling stressed is as follows:

● Breathe in. Hold for a count of three.

● When you breathe out again, say 'ten' at the same time, elongating the sound, letting go of tension as if it is being carried out of your body with the air.

● Next time you breathe out, say 'nine', and so on, all the way down to 'one'.

● When you get to 'one', start again.

● Each time you breathe out, tell yourself you are letting go of tension.

Many people repeat this sequence slowly for a period of 15–20 minutes. They find that with each new countdown, they reach a deeper level of relaxation.

3. Mindful breathing

You may find that this breathing exercise works for you.

- Sit comfortably.

- Listen to your breathing.

- Pay all your attention to your breath.

- Let any thoughts you have pass through. Acknowledge them but don't judge them.

- Keep your concentration on your breathing.

4. Guided imagery: Imagining a calm place

This is another very effective way of helping us to relax. With this method you imagine yourself in a place where you feel happy or peaceful. You can do this activity on your own or using an online guided meditation.

- Find a comfortable place free from distraction.

- Close your eyes.

- If you wish, you can play some soothing gentle music. It is probably better if you choose music with no lyrics.

- Imagine a place where you feel completely happy, relaxed and calm – your happy place. Perhaps it's your garden, your bedroom, a place where you had a great holiday, a favourite childhood spot. It could also be an imaginary setting, e.g. a tropical beach.

- Look around your happy place – take in what you are seeing, the colours and the shapes.

- Pay attention to the sounds you hear: listen carefully to the wind blowing, waves crashing, seagulls calling, etc.

- Reach out and touch things around you.

- Be aware of any smells.

- Now stay in this place for a while. Notice how relaxed you feel, how free of tension your body feels.

- Repeat in your head, 'I am relaxed, I am happy', 'I am a great person', 'Life is good'.

5. Progressive muscle relaxation

This relaxation technique helps with relaxing the body.

- Get comfortable. Lie on the floor or on a firm bed, or sit in a chair that has good support.

- Close your eyes and breathe deeply two or three times.

- Start with your face. Squint your eyes, tighten your jaws and wrinkle your forehead. Feel the tension while you count silently to five, and then let go of it. Feel the warmth of relaxation coming to your face.

- Next, pull your shoulders up until they nearly touch your ears. Feel the tension while you count silently to five. Then let go.

- Now continue down the rest of your body, tightening muscles as you go and counting slowly to five each time. Start with your hands, followed by your stomach, then work down to your thighs, and finish with your lower legs, tightening calf muscles and curling up your toes to feel and release the tension in your knees, calves, ankles and feet.

- When you have finished, notice the sense of release in all your muscles. Breathe deeply a few times, and then bring your attention back to the room.

Go to YouTube and look up '**#mindyourselfie Mindfulness Exercises**', which will bring up different relaxation techniques for you to follow.

6. Mindfulness colouring

Mindfulness colouring is a simple way of injecting a little calm into your day. The simple act of colouring brings your attention into the present moment. Why not try colouring in the illustration below the next time you're feeling stressed?

Knowing myself   Being healthy

INDIVIDUAL ACTIVITY

When you have completed one or a number of these exercises, answer these questions about it:

1. What was it like for you to do this exercise; did you find it easy or difficult? Why?

   _____

   _____

2. How did you feel after you had completed the exercise?

   _____

   _____

3. Can you think of situations in which this exercise might be helpful?

   _____

   _____

LEARNING KEEPSAKE

Three things I have learned in this lesson are:

1. _____

2. _____

3. _____

Something that helped me learn in this lesson was:

_____

_____

_____

As a result of this lesson, I will:

_____

_____

MEET THE CHALLENGE
Strand 4 Topic 1
MENTAL HEALTH LEAFLET

Learning outcomes: 1.1, 1.7, 4.3, 4.6, 4.9

Working in a group, design a mental health 'First Aid' leaflet for young people. Your leaflet should cover the following information:

○ Relaxation techniques

○ Contact details and information for different support agencies

○ Tips for maintaining positive mental health

○ Tips on how to manage stress

○ Tips on staying positive

○ Positive quotes

○ Ways to build self-esteem

○ Any other information that you feel is relevant

LESSON 32

Understanding Depression

Learning outcome: 4.5

 responsible resilient connected respected aware

By the end of this lesson you will:

• appreciate what it means to live with depression
• have identified ways of helping someone with depression
• understand the importance of getting help for depression

KEYWORDS

Depression

Bipolar disorder

Mild depression

Severe depression

Clinical depression

Seasonal affective disorder

 USEFUL WEBSITES

www.aware.ie Provides information and support for people who have depression.

What is depression?

Depression is a common mental health condition that affects 1 in 10 people in Ireland at any one time. That is nearly 450,000 people. It can vary from mild to severe and can have a serious effect on an individual and how they manage their daily lives. Depression can happen to anyone of any age, gender or background at any stage in their life. It is important to know that recovery is possible. Early recognition and ongoing support help the recovery process.

Thinking creatively and critically

CLASS ACTIVITY

Your teacher will read out the statements below that relate to depression. Hold up one hand if you agree, two hands if you disagree, or keep your hands down if you are unsure. (Alternatively, tick the box according to whether you agree, disagree or are unsure about each statement.)

STATEMENT	AGREE	DISAGREE	UNSURE
Depression happens when bad things happen in our lives, such as parents separating or bereavement.			
Depression is someone just feeling sorry for themselves; they could snap out of it if they really wanted to.			
Depression means that you are crazy.			
Depression will go away in time by itself if you wait long enough.			
People who experience depression need to take medication.			
People who are depressed are not sad all the time.			
Depression can go away and come back again.			
One in every five adolescents are likely to experience a depressive episode by the age of eighteen.			

The difference between feeling sad and being depressed

There are times when we feel sad and down. Sometimes this is because of a setback or disappointment. Usually these feelings don't last and we are back to normal in a few hours or days.

Some people, however, can find it difficult to escape this low mood. They can experience long-lasting feelings of sadness and hopelessness, or feel entirely numb, to the point where they find it difficult to take part in day-to-day activities. If this is the case, the person may be suffering from a medical condition known as clinical depression. Clinical depression is a treatable condition. It can affect people in different ways, and not everyone with depression will have the same symptoms, but it is important that a person seeks professional help if they have symptoms that last more than two weeks or if they have thoughts of self-harm or suicide.

Go to YouTube and look up 'I had a black dog, his name was Depression' (4:18) for an informative and straight-forward piece on what it feels like to have depression.

203

Symptoms of depression

The acronym **FESTIVAL**, despite its happy connotations, helps describe how depression can affect us.

Feeling: Depressed, sad, anxious, bored, or numb.

Energy: Low energy, tired or fatigued.

Sleep: Under- or over-sleeping, frequent waking during the night.

Thinking: Slow or negative thinking or poor concentration.

Interest: Loss of interest in school, hobbies, food, family.

Value: Low self-esteem, feeling worthless.

Aches: Physical aches and pains with no physical basis, e.g. chest/head/tummy pain associated with anxiety or stress.

Living: Loss of interest in living, thinking about death or suicide.

(Source: adapted from www.aware.ie)

Types of depression

The severity of depression depends on how much impact it has on a person's daily life.

Mild depression

Mild depression has some impact. With mild depression you might experience tiredness, early morning awakening, indecision, poor concentration and loss of confidence. A person experiencing mild depression may not notice they are depressed and may cope well in their daily lives.

Moderate depression

This type of depression has a significant impact. A person experiencing moderate depression may experience most of the symptoms listed for mild depression. It will also cause the person to be extremely tired, with their sleep being severely disturbed. Others can see this person is depressed.

Severe depression

A person experiencing severe depression will find it nearly impossible to get through daily life. As well as having the symptoms associated with moderate depression, this person will have a very negative opinion of their own self-worth. They will also have a very negative outlook for the future.

Bipolar disorder

Depression can sometimes occur as part of a related condition known as bipolar disorder. This disorder is characterised by periods of very low mood or depression and/or high mood or mania.

Post-natal depression (PND)

Some women experience this type of depression after childbirth. It can affect one in ten mothers and usually develops in the first four to six weeks after the child is born, although in some cases it might develop after several months.

Seasonal affective disorder (SAD)

SAD, also referred to as 'winter depression', is a type of depression that people can experience during the winter months.

Causes of depression

Depression can affect anyone and in some people it can happen suddenly and for no reason. However, there are some factors which make some people more at risk to depression.

Family history
Depression can sometimes run in families. This means that a person may be more susceptible to depression if a close relative has experienced it. However, it does not mean the person will definitely experience depression.

Personality
Certain personalities may be more vulnerable to experiencing depression. This includes people with low self-esteem who are overly critical of themselves..

Environmental factors
Stressful events can cause depression. These can include poverty, health issues, money worries, loneliness, unemployment, bereavement, divorce/separation, bullying.

Psychological factors
Severe trauma in childhood can cause depression. This includes child abuse (neglect, physical, emotional and sexual abuse). Loss in early childhood can also be a contributory factor.

Substance misuse
Alcohol and drug misuse can increase the risk of depression.

Seeking help when depressed

There are lots of different things that can help a person experiencing depression. Some of these you can do yourself and some you need support from others to do. Everyone's experience of mental health problems will be different, so what works for one person may not work for another person. You may need to try a number of options to see what works best for you.

Things you can do for yourself

Avoid alcohol

Alcohol is a depressant. If you're feeling down, it can make you feel worse. (Even if a person is not suffering from depression, alcohol often makes them feel down the following day.) The best advice would be to avoid alcohol if you are feeling depressed.

Keep a diary

Consider keeping a gratitude diary. Each evening, write down three good/nice things that happened that day, or three things you achieved that day, or three things you are grateful for, or a mixture of all three (it doesn't matter how small they are, or how seemingly insignificant; e.g. 'Mum made me a really nice dinner', 'I went for a ten-minute run', 'I'm grateful my grandad lives close by and I can visit him'). Although this may be difficult when you are feeling down, try to focus on what is going well in your life. This will help with your self-esteem.

Look after your physical health

There are lots of things you can do to help look after your mental health such as exercising, eating a balanced diet, sleeping, practising relaxation techniques and spending time with friends. If you have difficulty sleeping, think back to the tips for a good night's sleep you learned about in *My Wellbeing Journey 2*.

Talking

It is very important not to keep how you are feeling inside. Talk to a trusted adult or friend. Getting how you are feeling off your chest can make all the difference. Most people begin to feel better after opening up to someone they trust. Remember: 'A problem shared is a problem halved.' There are also a number of helplines listed in the 'Useful websites' section throughout this book that you can contact if you'd prefer to speak with someone anonymously.

Supports and services

If you think you are depressed and nothing you can do for yourself is helping, contact your doctor or mental health professional. They can help you get a correct diagnosis, advise you on what treatments are best for you and give you information about supports or services that can be of help.

There are a wide range of organisations and websites that can help people to deal with depression. Many of these services are low-cost or free. As well as the ones listed in the next lesson, the following two organisations provide helpful advice and information on coping with depression.

Aware This organisation offers information, support and education for people experiencing depression. It provides a range of services including group meetings, a helpline and email support service.

Website: www.aware.ie
Telephone: 1800 80 48 48
Email: supportmail@aware.ie

Health Service Executive The HSE has developed a website www.yourmentalhealth.ie that offers information on a wide range of issues related to mental health. This website enables you to search for services and supports in your local area.

How you can help someone who is depressed

If you suspect that a friend is affected by depression, you can be supportive by following this advice.

DO	DON'T
Take them seriously.	Make a joke of their situation.
Tell them you are there for them.	Tell them to pull themselves together.
Advise them to seek professional help.	Tell them you are just as depressed as they are.
Acknowledge their strengths in a specific way, e.g. 'You had two very good days last week.'	Tell them to stop feeling sorry for themselves.
Support them in healthy lifestyle choices, e.g. eating, exercising and relaxing.	Tell them to look at all the worse things that are happening to other people.
Offer your company and time.	Blame them – it is not their fault.
Remind them you can take care of yourself, they don't need to worry about upsetting you.	Avoid them.

 **INDIVIDUAL ACTIVITY**

Knowing myself

Being healthy

Read the following account from a person who experiences depression and answer the questions that follow.

MY ROAD TO RECOVERY

I have always been a quieter person, so when I started retreating into myself in Third Year, it seemed like no one noticed. I had many good friends, but at the time I thought I had no one. When friends used to ask how I was feeling I would just say, 'I'm fine, thanks.' They wouldn't enquire any further and I wouldn't reveal any more. I got about two to four hours of sleep each night, ate infrequently, felt worthless, and began to lose interest in everything – classes, friends, everything.

As time went on, I became more and more convinced that this was just how I was. I felt trapped and alone, like no one would understand what I was going through. I would think about asking for help and then be afraid about being a burden on my friends and family – constantly telling myself that they did not want me around or

that it would be better for them and for me if I wasn't around.

It continued like this, and my low mood and anxiety became so bad that I didn't want to do anything. In the mornings I was always worse. Some mornings I would wake up feeling like a fifty-pound weight had been placed on my chest. I was snapping at everyone. I felt like I couldn't speak to anyone. I thought I would look weak or stupid or crazy for talking about how I felt. I thought I *was* crazy. I began suffering from panic attacks but somehow managed to drag myself out of bed every day.

My parents had become aware by this point that I was struggling. One day I had a scheduled visit with my guidance counsellor, to discuss what subjects I would select for Fifth Year, and it was at this point that I broke down and told the counsellor

 207

that I was struggling and that I felt very low. The guidance counsellor contacted my mother and advised her to bring me to our GP. It was at this point that my journey to recovery began. I was diagnosed with depression and started treatment, visited a counsellor every week and began to really open up more. I started to share my feelings with family and friends. The counsellor gave me some coping skills to help me and I began to practise mindfulness every day. My friends really surprised me and were a great support once I opened up. I realised that they did care and that it was me that was shutting them out. They called more and sent me supportive texts. Now

I always talk to someone if I need help. It can be hard to talk to people, but if we all get better at talking about our feelings it can help to break down the mental health stigma. It is important to be there for one another; just someone to talk to when you are struggling can go a long way.

1. What signs were there that this person may have been experiencing depression?

   _____

   _____

2. Why do think they were reluctant to seek help?

   _____

   _____

3. If you knew this person and recognised that they were struggling, what would you do to support them?

   _____

   _____

4. What advice does the person in the story give to people who might be in a similar situation?

   _____

   _____

REMEMBER:

If you are concerned about any of the issues discussed in this lesson, make sure to talk to a trusted adult, a teacher or a counsellor in your school. They can offer you the help you need.

LEARNING KEEPSAKE

Three things I have learned in this lesson are:

1. _____

2. _____

3. _____

Something that helped me learn in this lesson was:

_____

_____

_____

As a result of this lesson, I will:

_____

_____

_____

LESSON 33 — Help Agencies

Learning outcome: 4.6

responsible   connected

By the end of this lesson you will:

↣ be familiar with some help agencies and how to contact them

INDIVIDUAL ACTIVITY

Being safe

How much do you know about the agencies that are out there to provide you with help, support and advice should you need it? Match the help agency to its logo by writing the number of the description in the box beside its logo.

1.	Offers advice and support to those who have been affected by alcohol problems.	**ISPCC** Childline	☐
2.	Offers support to people who are affected by eating disorders.	**SAMARITANS**	☐
3.	Offers support to people experiencing depression.	**SVP** Society of St Vincent de Paul	☐
4.	A HSE website that provides information on healthy relationships, consent and sexual health.	Rainbows Ireland — Supporting Children with Bereavement and Parental Separation	☐
5.	Telephone and email service for anyone who is struggling to cope day or night, 365 days a year.	Aware — Your supporting light through depression	☐
6.	Telephone and online services for children who need someone to listen.	b4udecide.ie — The Facts without the Lecture	☐

7.	Free community-based mental health service for 12–25-year-olds, offering one-to-one support for young people dealing with difficulties.	Supporting Lesbian, Gay, Bisexual & Trans Young People in Ireland **belong** ᵀᴼ	☐
8.	Offers support to young people who are grieving a death, separation or other painful transition in life.	**BODYWHYS** The Eating Disorders Association of Ireland	☐
9.	Supports lesbian, gay, bisexual, transgender and intersex (LGBTQ+) young people in Ireland.	**Al-Anon Family Groups** ▲◯	☐
10.	Dedicated to tackling poverty in all its forms.	**JIGSAW** Young people's health in mind	☐

PAIR ACTIVITY

Being safe

Learning with others

In pairs, read the following scenarios and answer the questions that follow.

Scenario 1: Family troubles

Robert's parents recently separated. Leading up to the separation his parents were arguing all the time. Now that Robert's father has left the family home, his mother is very upset and drinks regularly. Robert is really angry with his dad and won't speak to him. Robert has lost interest in his friends and his hobbies.

1. What agency do you think Robert can turn to for help?

_____

_____

2. What sort of support could they offer him?

_____

_____

3. Why might Robert be reluctant to seek help?

_____

_____

4. What sort of changes could occur in Robert's life if he seeks help?

_____

_____

Scenario 2: Confusing times

Jane is in Third Year in an all-girls' secondary school. Recently she has been confused about her sexuality: she has feelings towards one of the girls in her class.

1. What agency do you think Jane can turn to for help?

_____

_____

2. What sort of support could they offer her?

_____

_____

3. Why might Jane be reluctant to seek help?

_____

_____

4. What sort of changes could occur in Jane's life if she seeks help?

_____

_____

_____

Scenario 3: Exam stress

Joe is studying for his Junior Cycle exams. Despite working really hard, his class test results are not improving. His parents are really worried about him, but he feels nothing they do or say helps with his anxiety. His friends seem to get good grades with a fraction of the work he puts in. Joe feels under a lot of pressure.

1. What agency do you think Joe can turn to for help?

_____

_____

2. What sort of support could they offer him?

_____

_____

3. Why might Joe be reluctant to seek help?

_____

_____

4. What sort of changes could occur in Joe's life if he seeks help?

_____

_____

Scenario 4: Unplanned pregnancy

Last week Amy took a pregnancy test and it came up positive. She hasn't told anyone about the pregnancy and is terrified of what her parents will say. She feels alone and afraid.

1. What agency do you think Amy can turn to for help?

_____

_____

2. What sort of support could they offer her?

_____

_____

3. Why might Amy be reluctant to seek help?

_____

_____

4. What sort of changes could occur in Amy's life if she seeks help?

_____

_____

Contacting help agencies

Most help agencies have a website, a helpline or an email address. Before contacting an agency, be clear about what you want to say – writing it down might help you. Contact addresses and telephone numbers are available from:

- school guidance counsellors
- the telephone directory
- an internet search
- your GP

When you contact the organisation you will:

- speak to a trained counsellor who will listen to what you have to say
- be guaranteed confidentiality and anonymity
- be free to answer or not answer any questions that the counsellor may ask you – if you are not comfortable about answering a question, you can decide not to.

REMEMBER:
The best first step is to talk to a trusted adult. They will be able to support and help you.

INDIVIDUAL ACTIVITY

Evaluating information and data

Working on your own, select a help agency of your choice and design a business card for that agency to raise awareness in your school about the services the agency provides. Include the following details:

- name of the agency
- contact details
- the service it provides

Design your own logo for this help agency and include it in the business card design. When everyone in the class has completed their business card, put them together on a board for other students in the school to view.

LEARNING KEEPSAKE

Three things I have learned in this lesson are:

1. _____

2. _____

3. _____

Something that helped me learn in this lesson was:

_____

_____

_____

As a result of this lesson, I will:

_____

_____

_____

MEET THE CHALLENGE
Strand 4 Topic 2
WELLBEING WALL

Learning outcomes: 1.7, 2.1, 4.1, 4.6, 4.9

Your class has been given the task of designing and updating a 'Wellbeing Wall' for your school. This wall should provide positive, informative and encouraging messages about wellbeing. Create a space where everyone is welcome to read and contribute to the wall.

Suggestions for the wall:

- ◯ Tips for promoting positive mental health
- ◯ Stress busters
- ◯ Inspirational quotes and phrases
- ◯ Local and national help organisations
- ◯ Sticky notes section
- ◯ Healthy lifestyle tips (e.g. diet tips, exercise tips)
- ◯ Contact details for clubs in the local area to promote physical activity
- ◯ Any other information you think is necessary

SUPPORT GROUPS	HELPLINES
CARI: Children At Risk Ireland Provides support and counselling for children and families affected by sexual abuse. Tel: 1890 924 567	**Barnardos' Children's Bereavement Helpline Service** Helpline available from 10 a.m. to 12 p.m. Monday to Thursday to anyone seeking information and support in relation to bereavement. Tel: 01 473 2110
Jigsaw Ireland A free, community-based mental health service for 12–25-year-olds, offering one-to-one support for young people dealing with difficulties. www.jigsaw.ie	**BeLong To** A national online youth service for lesbian, gay, bisexual and transgender (LGBTQ+) young people in Ireland. www.belongto.org Tel: 01 670 6223
Rainbows Ireland A peer support group for people of all ages who have experienced death, separation or divorce in their lives. www.rainbowsireland.ie Tel: 01 473 4175	**Childline** A 24-hour helpline and online service offering advice and support to children and young people under 18. Freephone: 1800 666 666
Teen Between A specialised counselling service supprting teenagers with separated or divorced parents. Also offers a one-to-one counselling service. Freephone: 1800 303 191	**LGBTQ+ helpline** A non-judgemental and confidential helpline for LGBTQ+ people, their family and friends. Tel: 1890 929 539
	Samaritans A 24-hour helpline providing emotional support for people experiencing despair or distress. www.samaritans.org Freephone: 116 123
	TeenLine Ireland A helpline aimed at young people aged 13–19. www.teenline.ie Freephone: 1800 833 634